제대로
영작문

5

심화

장재영

유명 어학원과 영어학원에서 강의하면서 강사, 부원장, 원장을 역임.
(전) 리딩스타어학원 디렉터
(전) 청담어학원 원장
(전) 아발론교육 원장
(전) 고려대학교 국제어학원 영어교육프로그램 EiE 원장
(현) 슬기로운 영어학원 원장
특목고, 대학교 진로 진학 컨설팅

저서 『쓰담쓰담 내신영문법』 시리즈
　　　『시험에 강한 중학영문법』 시리즈

제대로 영작문 5 심화

지은이 장재영
펴낸이 정규도
펴낸곳 ㈜다락원

초판 1쇄 발행 2018년 1월 2일
개정판 2쇄 발행 2024년 6월 27일

편집 김민아, 홍인표
디자인 구수정, 황수영
영문 감수 Mark Holden
일러스트 윤미선

🏢 다락원 경기도 파주시 문발로 211
내용 문의 (02)736-2031 내선 504
구입 문의 (02)736-2031 내선 250~252
Fax (02)732-2037
출판 등록 1977년 9월 16일 제406-2008-000007호
Copyright © 2024 장재영

ISBN 978-89-277-8076-2 54740
　　　978-89-277-8071-7 54740 (set)

www.darakwon.co.kr
다락원 홈페이지를 방문하시면 상세한 출판정보와 함께 동영상강좌, MP3 자료 등 다양한 어학 정보를 얻으실 수 있습니다.

제대로 영작문

5

심화

DARAKWON

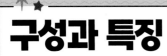

구성과 특징

서술형·수행평가 만점을 만드는
제대로 영작문·5

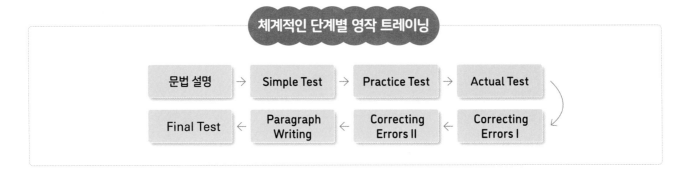

체계적인 단계별 영작 트레이닝

문법 설명 → Simple Test → Practice Test → Actual Test

Final Test ← Paragraph Writing ← Correcting Errors II ← Correcting Errors I

How to Study

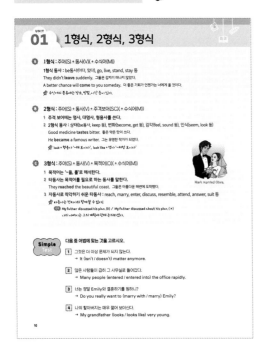

1 문법 설명

영작에 꼭 필요한 핵심 문법을 재미있는 삽화와
암기 팁 등과 함께 공부할 수 있습니다.

2 Simple Test

간단한 빈칸 채우기 문제로 문법에 대한 이해도를 확인합니다.

3 Practice Test

주어진 단어를 활용하여 비교적 짧고 쉬운 문장을
써 보는 연습 문제입니다.

4 Actual Test

이제는 비교적 어려운 문장도 영작해보면서 문장을 자기 것으로 만듭니다.

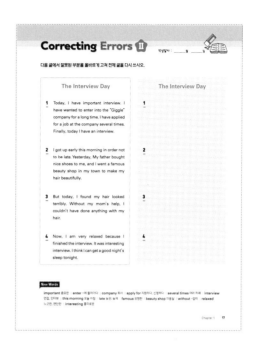

5 Correcting Errors I

우리말과 같은 뜻이 되도록 문장을 바르게 고친 후,
전체 문장을 다시 써 봅니다.

6 Correcting Errors II

주어진 글에서 틀린 부분을 모두 찾아 고친 후,
전체 글을 다시 써 봅니다.

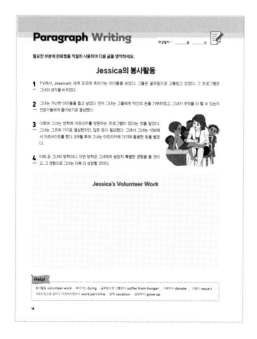

8 Final Test

모든 Chapter의 학습을 마친 후 앞서 배운 내용을 최종 점검합니다.
내신 서술형 평가와 수행평가는 물론 수능 어법 유형까지
제대로 대비하세요!

7 Paragraph Writing

Chapter가 끝날 때마다 배운 문법을 최대한 활용하여
다양한 에세이를 써 봅니다.

목차

Chapter

1

문장의 형식

UNIT 01 1형식, 2형식, 3형식

A **1형식** : 주어(S) + 동사(V)(+ 수식어(M))

1형식 동사 : be동사(이다, 있다), go, live, stand, stay 등

They didn't **leave** suddenly. 그들은 갑자기 떠나지 않았다.

A better chance will **come** to you someday. 더 좋은 기회가 언젠가는 너에게 올 것이다.

📌 수식어의 종류에는 장소, 방법, 시간 등이 있다.

B **2형식** : 주어(S) + 동사(V) + 주격보어(SC)(+ 수식어(M))

1 주격 보어에는 명사, 대명사, 형용사를 쓴다.

2 2형식 동사 : 상태(be동사, keep 등), 변화(become, get 등), 감각(feel, sound 등), 인식(seem, look 등)

Good medicine **tastes** bitter. 좋은 약은 맛이 쓰다.

He **became** a famous writer. 그는 유명한 작가가 되었다.

📌 look + 형용사 '~해 보이다', look like + 명사 '~처럼 보이다'

Mark married Olivia.

C **3형식** : 주어(S) + 동사(V) + 목적어(O)(+ 수식어(M))

1 목적어는 '~을, 를'로 해석한다.

2 타동사는 목적어를 필요로 하는 동사를 말한다.

They **reached** the beautiful coast. 그들은 아름다운 해변에 도착했다.

3 자동사로 착각하기 쉬운 타동사 : reach, marry, enter, discuss, resemble, attend, answer, suit 등

📌 타동사는 전치사와 함께 쓸 수 없다!

ex My father discussed his plan. (O) / My father discussed about his plan. (✕)

나의 아버지는 그의 계획에 관해 논의하셨다.

Simple Test

다음 중 어법에 맞는 것을 고르시오.

1 그것은 더 이상 문제가 되지 않는다.

→ It (isn't / doesn't) matter anymore.

2 많은 사람들이 급히 그 사무실로 들어갔다.

→ Many people (entered / entered into) the office rapidly.

3 너는 정말 Emily와 결혼하기를 원하니?

→ Do you really want to (marry with / marry) Emily?

4 나의 할아버지는 매우 젊어 보이신다.

→ My grandfather (looks / looks like) very young.

Practice Test

정답 p.02

What's your score? O   개 X   개

다음 괄호 안의 주어진 단어를 이용하여 문장을 완성하세요.

1 그 의사는 그 간호사와 결혼했다. (marry)

_____

2 모든 사람이 그 결과를 보자마자 창백해졌다. (turn, pale, upon seeing, result)

_____

3 서울(Seoul)에서 가장 큰 나무가 저 언덕 위에 서 있다. (stand, hill, big)

_____

4 그들은 그것의 진짜 가치를 몰랐다. (real, value)

_____

5 그들은 이웃들과 좋은 관계를 유지했다. (neighbors, keep, with)

_____

6 다음 기차는 오후 2시에 도착할 것이다. (will, arrive)

_____

7 많은 사람들이 오늘 투표하는 것을 포기했다. (give up, voting)

_____

8 우리에게는 단 한 번의 기회가 있을 것이다. (there, just, opportunity)

_____

9 이 오래된 우표는 매우 가치 있는 것 같다. (seem, valuable)

_____

10 그들의 대표자가 그 회담에 참여했다. (attend, representative, conference)

_____

Actual Test

정답 p.02

What's your score? O   개   X   개

다음 괄호 안의 주어진 단어를 이용하여 문장을 완성하세요.

1 이 보고서에 따르면, 우리는 더 좋은 방법을 찾을 수 없다. (according to, way)

_____

2 우리는 오늘 객관식 시험만을 치를 것이다. (have, only, multiple choice test)

_____

3 이 모자는 너의 머리에 너무 작아 보인다. (look, for)

_____

4 우리는 두 시간 후에 방콕(Bangkok)에 도착할 예정이다. (going to, in)

_____

5 이 카페의 카푸치노는 맛이 환상적이다. (the cappuccino, taste)

_____

6 이렇게 아름다운 장소에서는 누구나 시인이 될 수 있다. (everyone, poet, in, place)

_____

7 많은 교수님들이 어제 그 회의에 참석했다. (professor, attend)

_____

8 그들은 허락도 없이 그 방에 들어갔다. (without, get permission)

_____

9 오늘 아침에 회의가 3시간 동안 계속되었다. (last)

_____

10 우리는 그 문제를 매우 심각하게 논의했다. (discuss, matter)

_____

New Words

bitter 맛이 쓴 | reach ~에 도착하다 | matter 문제가 되다; 문제 | rapidly 급히 | pale 창백한 | on [upon] -ing ~하자마자 곧 |
vote 투표하다 | opportunity 기회 | valuable 가치 있는 | representative 대표(자) | conference 회의, 회담 | according to
~에 따르면 | multiple choice test 객관식 시험 | poet 시인 | permission 허락 | last 계속되다, 지속하다

UNIT 02 4형식, 5형식

A **4형식** : 주어(S) + 동사(V) + 간접목적어(IO) + 직접목적어(DO)

1 수여동사는 주로 '주다'의 의미를 가진 4형식 동사를 말한다.

Encouragement **gives us courage**. 격려는 우리에게 용기를 준다.

2 4형식 문장에서 3형식 문장으로의 전환

· 주어(S) + 동사(V) + 직접목적어(DO) + **전치사(to/for/of)** + 간접목적어(IO)

전치사	구분	동사
to	방향, 대상	give, send, show, tell, lend, teach, promise 등
for	이익	make, buy, cook, get, find, choose, call, order, prepare 등
of	요청	ask, inquire, require, beg 등

This experiment may not **give us a good result**. (4형식)

→ This experiment may not **give a good result to us**. (3형식)
이 실험은 우리에게 좋은 결과를 주지 않을지도 모른다.

📌 explain, describe, mention 등은 4형식 문장에는 쓸 수 없고 3형식 문장에만 쓴다.

B **5형식** : 주어(S) + 동사(V) + 목적어(O) + 목적격 보어(OC)

1 목적격 보어는 목적어의 상태를 보충해주는 말이다.

2 목적격 보어에는 (대)명사, 형용사, 분사, (원형)부정사 등을 쓴다.

3 5형식 대표 동사 : make, let, have, get, help, call, leave, name, think, believe, find, consider 등

Doing nothing **makes people stupid**. 아무것도 안 하는 것은 사람들을 멍청하게 한다. (형용사)

He **made his students study** hard. 그는 학생들을 열심히 공부하게 했다. (원형부정사 = 동사원형)

📌 사역동사 : have, let, make + 목적어 + 동사원형
준사역동사 : get + 목적어 + to부정사 / help + 목적어 + to부정사 또는 동사원형
지각동사 : see, watch, hear, feel 등 + 목적어 + 동사원형 또는 -ing

Simple Test

다음 중 어법에 맞는 것을 고르시오.

1 나의 아이들은 항상 나에게 기쁨을 준다. (4형식)
→ My kids always give (happiness me / me happiness).

2 나의 아버지는 나에게 새 휴대전화를 사 주셨다. (3형식)
→ My father bought a new cell phone (to / for) me.

3 그들은 그에게 중요한 질문을 했다. (3형식)
→ They asked an important question (to / of) him.

4 아름다운 노래들은 우리를 편안하게 해준다. (5형식)
→ Beautiful songs make us (comfortable / comfortably).

Practice Test

정답 p.02

What's your score? O   개 X   개

다음 괄호 안의 주어진 단어와 조건을 이용하여 문장을 완성하세요.

1 그 유명한 골프선수가 나에게 골프공 하나를 주었다. (golfer, 4형식)

_____

2 그들은 마침내 그에게 자유를 주었다. (finally, 3형식)

_____

3 좋은 습관들은 우리를 부지런하게 한다. (habit, make)

_____

4 그 가게 주인은 나에게 좋은 과일들을 골라 주었다. (storekeeper, choose, 3형식)

_____

5 Sally는 모든 심사위원들 앞에서 좋은 공연을 하였다. (judges, give, all of, 3형식)

_____

6 내가 당신에게 부탁 하나 해도 될까요? (ask, favor, 4형식)

_____

7 돈은 때때로 사람들을 슬프게 한다. (sometimes, make)

_____

8 내가 어제 무엇을 했는지 설명해 줄게. (let, what, explain)

_____

9 우리를 지금 집에 가게 해 줘. (let)

_____

10 나는 한국 드라마가 환상적이라고 생각한다. (fantastic, 5형식)

_____

Actual Test

정답 p.02

What's your score? O   개   X   개

다음 괄호 안의 주어진 단어와 조건을 이용하여 문장을 완성하세요.

1 그들은 그 고아원에 많은 선물을 주었다. (orphanage, 3형식)

_____

2 견과류를 먹는 것은 사람들을 훨씬 더 건강하게 한다. (eating nuts, make, much)

_____

3 이 새 기계는 우리의 업무를 더 쉽게 만들 것이다. (make, work)

_____

4 배드민턴을 치는 것이 우리 부모님을 훨씬 더 활기차게 한다. (playing, make, active, much)

_____

5 속담들은 우리에게 좋은 교훈을 줄 것이다. (proverbs, lessons, 4형식)

_____

6 늦게까지 깨어있는 것은 우리를 피곤하게 한다. (staying up, make)

_____

7 그 정부는 그 행사를 월드마켓(The World Market)이라고 이름 지었다. (the government, name)

_____

8 많은 사람들이 그의 발명을 기적이라고 생각했다. (invention, miracle, 5형식)

_____

9 그는 나에게 이 혼란스러운 상황을 설명하지 않았다. (confusing, situation, 3형식)

_____

10 그 코치는 Sam이 최고의 선수라고 생각했다. (best player, 5형식)

_____

New Words

encouragement 격려, 응원 | courage 용기 | experiment 실험 | finally 마침내 | habit 습관 | storekeeper 가게 주인 |
give a performance 공연을 하다 | judge 심사위원 | favor 호의, 친절 | orphanage 고아원 | proverb 속담 | stay up late (안자고)
늦게까지 깨어 있다 | government 정부 | invention 발명 | confusing 혼란스러운 | situation 상황

Correcting Errors ⭐

What's your score? O   개   X   개

다음 우리말과 같은 뜻이 되도록 어색한 부분을 바르게 고쳐 문장을 다시 쓰시오.

1   The students entered into their classroom quickly.

→ _____

그 학생들은 빨리 그들의 교실로 들어갔다.

2   He looks very sadly today because of bad news.

→ _____

그는 오늘 나쁜 소식 때문에 매우 슬퍼 보인다.

3   She bought a beautiful house to her mother.

→ _____

그녀는 그녀의 어머니에게 아름다운 집을 사드렸다.

4   The teacher asked tough questions to his pupils.

→ _____

그 선생님은 그의 제자들에게 어려운 질문들을 했다.

5   He had his daughter did her homework.

→ _____

그는 그의 딸이 자신의 숙제를 하게 했다.

6   They saw the girls danced on the stage.

→ _____

그들은 그 소녀들이 무대에서 춤을 추는 것을 보았다.

7   Can you give the report us?

→ _____

너는 그 보고서를 우리에게 줄 수 있니?

8   She looks like very tired today.

→ _____

그녀는 오늘 매우 피곤해 보인다.

Correcting Errors II

작성일자 : _____월 _____일

다음 글에서 잘못된 부분을 올바르게 고쳐 전체 글을 다시 쓰시오.

The Interview Day

1 Today, I have important interview. I have wanted to enter into the "Giggle" company for a long time. I have applied for a job at the company several times. Finally, today I have an interview.

2 I got up early this morning in order not to be late. Yesterday, My father bought nice shoes to me, and I went a famous beauty shop in my town to make my hair beautifully.

3 But today, I found my hair looked terribly. Without my mom's help, I couldn't have done anything with my hair.

4 Now, I am very relaxed because I finished the interview. It was interesting interview. I think I can get a good night's sleep tonight.

The Interview Day

1

2

3

4

New Words

important 중요한 | enter ~에 들어가다 | company 회사 | apply for 지원하다, 신청하다 | several times 여러 차례 | interview 면접, 인터뷰 | this morning 오늘 아침 | late 늦은; 늦게 | famous 유명한 | beauty shop 미용실 | without ~없이 | relaxed 느긋한, 편안한 | interesting 흥미로운

Paragraph Writing

여러 형식의 문장들을 적절히 사용하여 다음 글을 영작하세요.

Jessica의 봉사활동

1 TV에서, Jessica는 세계 곳곳에 죽어가는 아이들을 보았다. 그들은 굶주림으로 고통받고 있었다. 그 프로그램은 그녀의 생각을 바꾸었다.

2 그녀는 가난한 아이들을 돕고 싶었다. 먼저 그녀는 그들에게 약간의 돈을 기부하였고, 그녀가 무엇을 더 할 수 있는지 전문가들에게 물어보기로 결심했다.

3 이후에 그녀는 방학에 아프리카를 방문하는 프로그램이 있다는 것을 알았다. 그녀는 그곳에 가기로 결심했지만, 많은 돈이 필요했다. 그래서 그녀는 식당에서 아르바이트를 했다. 3개월 후에 그녀는 아프리카에 가기에 충분한 돈을 벌었다.

4 이제 곧 그녀의 방학이다. 이번 방학은 그녀에게 굉장히 특별한 경험을 줄 것이고, 그 경험으로 그녀는 더욱 더 성장할 것이다.

Jessica's Volunteer Work

Help!

봉사활동 volunteer work | 죽어가는 dying | 굶주림으로 고통받다 suffer from hunger | 기부하다 donate | 전문가 expert | 파트타임으로 일하다, 아르바이트하다 work part-time | 방학 vacation | 성장하다 grow up

Chapter

2

명사절과
부사절

A 접속사 that이 이끄는 명사절

1 주어의 역할을 하는 경우

That I felt in love with her is unforgettable. 그녀를 사랑했던 것을 나는 잊지 못한다.

= **It** is unforgettable **that I felt in love with her**.
　가주어　　　　　　　　　　　　　진주어

2 목적어의 역할을 하는 경우 : 이때, that은 생략 가능하다.

I think **(that) you can achieve your goal soon**. 나는 네가 너의 목표를 곧 이룰 수 있다고 생각한다.
　　　　　　　　　　목적어

📌 that절을 목적어로 취하는 주요 동사 : tell, say, believe, think, know, hope, admit 등

3 보어의 역할을 하는 경우

The best way to solve this problem is **that we cooperate with each other**.
　　　　　　　　　　　　　　　　　　　　　　　보어

이 문제를 해결하는 가장 좋은 방법은 우리가 서로 협동하는 것이다.

4 동격의 that절 : 앞선 명사와 동격의 역할을 한다.

The thought **that** many Koreans like coffee is not surprising now.
많은 한국 사람들이 커피를 좋아한다는 생각은 이제 놀랍지 않다.

📌 동격절을 이끄는 주요 명사 : fact, news, belief, opinion, idea, thought, hope, advice, doubt, question, feeling, decision 등

B 접속사 whether / if가 이끄는 명사절 📌 '~인지 아닌지'

1 whether : 주어, 목적어, 보어 역할이 모두 가능하다.

Whether he can do it (or not) is not important to you.
그가 그것을 했는지 안 했는지는 너에게 중요하지 않다.

2 if : 문장에서 동사의 목적어로만 쓰인다.

I wonder **if** you are willing to participate in the meeting (or not).
네가 회의에 기꺼이 참여할지 안 할지 궁금하다.

whether or not (O)
if or not (X)

Simple Test

다음 중 어법에 맞는 것을 고르시오.

1 그것이 그의 잘못이었다는 것은 명백하다. → It is obvious (that / if) it was his fault.

2 나는 그들이 그 땅을 소유하고 있는지 아닌지 모른다.
　→ I don't know (that / if) they own the land or not.

3 그 로봇이 움직이는지 아닌지는 알려지지 않았다.
　→ (If / Whether) the robot can move is not known.

4 그가 저격수라는 사실은 일급비밀이다.
　→ The fact (that / whether) he is a sniper is top secret.

Practice Test

What's your score? O   개   X   개

다음 괄호 안의 주어진 단어를 이용하여 문장을 완성하세요.

1 우리는 그들이 안전하게 돌아오기를 희망한다. (hope, safely)

_____

2 그녀가 일본 출신인지 아닌지는 중요하지 않다. (from)

_____

3 그녀는 그들이 좋은 사람인지 아닌지를 의심했다. (doubt, good people)

_____

4 그녀의 취미가 동전 모으기라는 것은 놀랍다. (that, surprising, collecting)

_____

5 커피가 당신의 건강에 좋다는 생각은 이상하다. (idea, good, strange)

_____

6 나는 우리가 여기를 탈출할 수 있을 것이라고 믿어. (escape, that)

_____

7 나는 그녀가 저 높은 산을 올라갈 수 있을지 궁금하다. (wonder, climb, can)

_____

8 지하철 요금을 인상했다는 뉴스는 매우 실망스럽다. (fare, news, increase, disappointing)

_____

9 주요 쟁점은 교수들이 연구할 충분한 시간이 없다는 것이다. (main, issue, to study)

_____

10 그 회사가 많은 문제를 가지고 있다는 사실은 더 이상 안 알려져 있지 않다. (firm, fact, unknown)

_____

What's your score? O 개 X 개

다음 괄호 안의 주어진 단어를 이용하여 문장을 완성하세요.

1 그가 테니스 선수인지 아닌지는 수수께끼이다. (tennis player, or, riddle)

_____

2 그가 우리의 적이라는 생각은 매우 위험하다. (thought, enemy)

_____

3 James가 해산물을 먹는 것은 매우 이례적이다. (it, exceptional, for, seafood)

_____

4 일기예보에서는 비가 온다고 했기 때문에 나는 내 차를 세차해야 하는지 확신하지 못한다.
(sure, should, forecast, call for)

_____

5 나의 주된 관심은 그 외국인들이 한국어를 말할 수 있는지 없는 지이다. (concern, foreigners)

_____

6 그 가수가 결혼했다는 사실은 알려지지 않았다. (fact, married, known)

_____

7 나는 그녀가 많이 먹는지 아닌지 궁금하다. (wonder, a lot, or not)

_____

8 요즈음에는 사람들이 인터넷에서 뉴스를 읽는 것이 보편적이다. (it, that, these days, universal, on)

_____

9 인류가 오래 전에 원숭이로부터 진화했다는 이론은 그럴듯하게 들린다. (theory, plausible, sound)

_____

10 어린이들이 항상 이리저리 뛰어다니는 것은 당연하다. (it, here and there, natural, that, all the time)

_____

New Words

unforgettable 잊을 수 없는 | cooperate 협력하다 | participate in ~에 참여하다 | be willing to 기꺼이 ~하다 | obvious 분명한, 명백한 | fault 잘못, 책임 | sniper 저격수 | strange 이상한, 낯선 | fare 운임, 요금 | riddle 수수께끼 | exceptional 예외적인, 이례적인 | forecast 일기예보 | call for (날씨를) 예상하다 | concern 관심, 염려 | universal 보편적인, 일반적인 | theory 이론 | evolve 진화하다 | plausible 그럴듯한 | natural 당연한 | here and there 이리저리

UNIT 04 부사절

A 시간의 부사절

시간을 나타내는 접속사

when	~할 때	until	~할 때까지
while	~하는 동안	once	일단 ~하면
as	~하고 있을 때, ~하면서	not A until B	B하고 나서야 비로소 A하다
since	~한 이래로	as soon as	~하자마자

When people are hungry, they usually get sensitive. 사람들은 배고플 때 흔히 예민해진다.

B 이유의 부사절

이유를 나타내는 접속사 : because, since, as '~이기 때문에'

As he hadn't saved enough money, he couldn't buy new shoes today.
그는 충분한 돈을 저금하지 않았기 때문에 오늘 새 신발을 살 수 없었다.

C 조건의 부사절

조건을 나타내는 접속사 : if '만약 ~라면', unless '만약 ~이 아니라면', as long as '~하는 한'

Unless Harry's car works well, he will repair it.
만약 Harry의 차가 잘 작동하지 않는다면 그는 그것을 수리할 것이다.

D 양보의 부사절

양보를 나타내는 접속사 : though, although, even though (사실), even if (가정) '~에도 불구하고, 비록 ~일지라도'

Although the weather was terrible, they decided to hold the festival.
날씨가 지독히 좋지 않았어도 그들은 축제를 열기로 했다.

E 목적, 결과의 부사절 📌 so that, in order that '~하기 위하여'

He practiced for over 10 hours a day **so that** he could be an expert in that field.
그는 그 분야에서 전문가가 되기 위해서 하루에 10시간 이상 연습했다.

Simple Test

다음 중 어법에 맞는 것을 고르시오.

1 선생님께 혼이 났음에도 불구하고 그녀는 미소를 지었다.
→ She smiled (since / though) she got scolded by her teacher.

2 그 할머니는 나를 보자마자 나를 따뜻하게 안아주셨다.
→ (As soon as / Once) the old woman saw me, she hugged me warmly.

3 그것은 내가 이 학교에 들어온 이후로 가장 충격적인 뉴스였다.
→ It was the most shocking news (until / since) I entered this school.

Practice Test

What's your score? O   개   X   개

다음 괄호 안의 주어진 단어를 이용하여 문장을 완성하세요.

1 만약 그가 바쁘지 않다면 나는 그의 도움을 청할 것이다. (unless, ask for, help)

_____

2 백설공주(Snow White)는 사과 하나를 먹자마자 깊이 잠이 들었다. (fall deeply asleep)

_____

3 그는 배가 불렀기 때문에 더 이상 아무것도 먹을 수 없었다. (full, since, anything)

_____

4 그녀가 창문을 열었을 때 그녀는 상쾌한 바람을 느낄 수 있었다. (as, refreshing wind)

_____

5 안개가 걷힐 때까지 그 배들은 출항할 수 없었다. (fog, clear, sail)

_____

6 내가 Billy를 용서했을 때 그는 이미 한국을 떠났다. (forgive, had, left)

_____

7 그가 내게 전화를 걸었을 때 나는 그의 힘없는 목소리에 매우 놀랐다. (surprised, at, weak)

_____

8 공기는 귀중함에도 우리는 무료로 그것을 들이마실 수 있다. (valuable, breathe ~ in, for free)

_____

9 그 뚱뚱한 남자는 식사를 하는 동안 계속해서 땀을 흘렸다. (while, have a meal, keep, sweat)

_____

10 그 교수님이 학생들의 이름을 부르는 동안 나는 조용히 자리에 앉았다. (was calling, on my seat)

_____

Actual Test ✩✩

정답 p.05

What's your score? O   개 X   개

다음 괄호 안의 주어진 단어를 이용하여 문장을 완성하세요.

1 그는 부산(Busan)에 갈 때마다 회를 먹는다. (whenever, raw fish)

_____

2 내 남동생은 집에 도착하자마자 화장실로 급히 갔다. (get, rush to)

_____

3 그녀는 지갑을 잃어버리고 나서 그것을 찾기 위해 주위를 둘러보았다. (her wallet, look around for)

_____

4 그는 그 소문을 듣자마자 그것을 그의 친구들에게 말했다. (hear, rumor, as, tell)

_____

5 내가 살아있는 한 이 회사를 팔지 않을 것이다. (long, alive, firm)

_____

6 진수(Jinsu)는 기타를 잘 치기 때문에 많은 소녀들이 그를 좋아한다. (since, many, good at)

_____

7 많은 모기들이 있기 때문에 우리는 그 집에서 잘 수 없다. (because, there, mosquito)

_____

8 그 선생님이 나에게 질문을 할 때 나는 항상 긴장된다. (when, nervous)

_____

9 일단 네가 그 식당을 방문하면 그 음식 맛에 만족할 것이다. (once, satisfied with, taste)

_____

10 그 아이들은 물에서 노는 것을 좋아했기 때문에 그 욕조에서 나오지 않았다.
(because, tub, come out of, playing)

_____

New Words

sensitive 예민한, 민감한 | expert 전문가 | get scolded 혼나다, 야단맞다 | shocking 충격적인 | refreshing 상쾌한 |
fall asleep 잠들다 | clear (구름·안개가) 걷히다, 개다 | breathe something in ~을 들이마시다 | sweat 땀을 흘리다 |
raw fish 날 생선, 생선회 | bathroom 화장실 | look around for ~을 찾기 위해 둘러보다 | mosquito 모기 | taste 맛 | tub 욕조

Correcting Errors ❶

정답 p.05

What's your score? O   개 X   개

다음 우리말과 같은 뜻이 되도록 어색한 부분을 바르게 고쳐 문장을 다시 쓰시오.

1 I wonder that she likes me or not.

→ _____

나는 그녀가 나를 좋아하는지 아닌지 궁금하다.

2 They are not polite is very disappointing.

→ _____

그들이 예의 바르지 않다는 것은 매우 실망스럽다.

3 We just stayed inside though the weather was very bad.

→ _____

날씨가 매우 안 좋았기 때문에 우리는 실내에 머물렀다.

4 Because I was full, I had more dessert.

→ _____

배가 불렀지만 나는 간식을 더 먹었다.

5 He exercises every morning in order to he loses weight.

→ _____

그는 살을 빼기 위해 매일 아침 운동을 한다.

6 Unless he didn't save the money, he couldn't buy anything.

→ _____

그 돈을 저축하지 않았다면, 그는 아무것도 살 수 없었다.

7 It is very clear which he can't go abroad by himself.

→ _____

그 혼자서 외국으로 갈 수 없다는 것은 매우 명백하다.

8 The idea what people can't live without water is not strange.

→ _____

사람들이 물 없이는 살 수 없다는 생각은 이상하지 않다.

Correcting Errors

작성일자 : _____월 _____일

다음 글에서 잘못된 부분을 올바르게 고쳐 전체 글을 다시 쓰시오.

The Special Prize

1 It is fantastic that my older sister won first prize in the writing contest.

2 As long as she got home, she told us about winning first prize. We congratulated her on winning it. If she is the best or not is not important for me.

3 My concern is what the prize is very special. It is a brand-new smartphone! But she bought the latest model a few days ago.

4 I have used my cell phone for over three years. I want to change my cell phone. But I am not sure if or not my father and older sister will agree with my idea.

The Special Prize

1

2

3

4

New Words

win first prize 1등 상을 타다 | contest 대회, 시합 | concern 관심, 걱정 | brand-new 아주 새로운, 신형의 | latest 최근의, 최신의 | special 특별한 | cell phone 휴대전화 | be sure 확신하다 | agree 동의하다

Paragraph Writing

작성일자 : _____월 _____일

필요한 부분에 명사절과 부사절을 적절히 사용하여 다음 글을 영작하세요.

한국 드라마

1 한국 드라마가 흥미롭다는 사실은 이미 잘 알려져 있다. 드라마를 만드는 많은 TV 방송국들이 있기 때문에 사람들은 여러 가지 좋은 드라마를 고를 수 있다.

2 일단 한 편의 드라마를 보기 시작하면, 우리는 마지막 편까지 그것을 시청한다. 첫 회 이후에 시청자들은 그 드라마가 성공할지 아닐지를 알 수 있다. 첫 회가 시청률이 높으면, 더 많은 사람들이 그 드라마에 관심을 가지게 된다.

3 첫 에피소드 전에 많은 배우들은 시청률 공략을 한다. 만약 시청률이 어떤 수준에 도달하면, 그들은 그들의 팬들에게 보답하는 무언가를 할 것을 약속한다. 어떤 배우들은 우스꽝스러운 의상을 입고 거리를 걷고, 어떤 배우들은 사인회를 가지기도 한다.

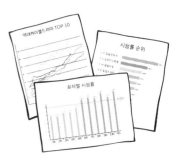

4 좋은 드라마들이 한국에 있는 한, 더 많은 배우들이 그들의 기량을 계속 개발할 수 있다.

Korean Dramas

Help!

well known 잘 알려진, 유명한 | broadcasting station 방송국 | the last episode 마지막 회 | viewer 시청자 | ratings 시청률 | make a pledge 서약하다, 맹세하다 | repay 보답하다 | ridiculous 우스꽝스러운 | costume 복장 | have a signing event 사인회를 가지다

Chapter

3

관계사

UNIT 05 관계대명사

A who, whose, who(m) : 선행사가 사람일 때

who	주격	선행사가 관계대명사 뒤 내용의 주어 역할을 한다.
		The woman **who** is sitting on the bench is my math teacher. 그 벤치에 앉아 있는 여자는 우리 수학 선생님이야.
whose	소유격	선행사가 관계대명사 뒤 내용의 소유격 역할을 한다.
		Michael **whose** father is a novelist is my best friend. 아버지가 소설가인 Michael이 나의 가장 친한 친구야.
who(m)	목적격	선행사가 관계대명사 뒤 내용의 목적격 역할을 한다.
		Terry **who(m)** Julie fell in love with last year will leave Korea soon. 작년에 Julie가 사랑에 빠진 Terry는 곧 한국을 떠날 것이다. (Terry는 전치사 with의 목적어)

B which, whose, which : 선행사가 사물일 때

which	주격	I want to buy a new watch **which** will help me to work effectively. 일을 효율적으로 하도록 도울 새 시계를 사고 싶다.
whose	소유격	This is a special robot **whose** value is not known yet. 이 특별한 로봇의 가치는 아직 알려지지 않았다. 📌 whose는 선행사가 사물일 때도 사용 가능하다.
which	목적격	I don't like the bag **which** my father bought yesterday. 어제 아버지께서 사오신 가방을 나는 좋아하지 않는다.

the bag which my father bought

C what : 선행사를 포함한 관계대명사 (= the thing(s) that [which])

I really want to know **what** you did this morning. 나는 오늘 아침에 네가 무엇을 했는지 정말 알고 싶다.

D 관계대명사 that만 써야 하는 경우

1 선행사에 사람, 동물(사물)이 함께 있을 때
Look at the girl and her dog **that** are running. 뛰고 있는 그 소녀와 강아지를 봐.

2 선행사에 -thing, very, all, every, any, no, little, the only 등이 있을 때
That is **something** special **that** we've never experienced before. 전에 결코 경험하지 못한 특별한 뭔가가 있다.

E 관계대명사의 계속적 용법

1 관계대명사 앞에 쉼표(,)를 쓰고, 「접속사 + 대명사」로 바꿔 쓸 수 있다.
The employer hired two employees, **who** are very diligent. 사장은 두 명의 직원을 고용했는데, 그들은 매우 부지런하다.
= The employer hired two employees, **and they** are very diligent.

2 that과 what은 계속적 용법으로 쓸 수 없다. ex 쉼표(,) + that (X) / 쉼표(,) + what (X)

Simple Test

다음 중 어법에 맞는 것을 고르시오.

1 나는 위대한 곡들을 작곡했던 베토벤(Beethoven)을 존경한다.
→ I admire Beethoven (who / which) composed great songs.

2 그가 사고 싶어 하는 것은 새 자전거이다. → (That / What) he wants to buy is a new bicycle.

Practice Test

다음 괄호 안의 주어진 단어를 이용하여 문장을 완성하세요.

1   나는 매우 공격적인 고양이를 봤다. (which, aggressive, see)

_____

2   나는 2주 전에 키가 매우 큰 나의 삼촌을 만났다. (who, ago)

_____

3   눈이 큰 그 아이는 나를 보고 웃고 있었다. (child, whose, big, at)

_____

4   네가 어젯밤에 한 일은 정말 멋졌다. (what, terrific)

_____

5   이것은 내가 그 대회에서 받은 1등 상이야. (prize, win, in the contest)

_____

6   그는 돌이킬 수 없는 실수를 저질렀다. (mistake, irrevocable, which)

_____

7   저 은행 앞에 서 있는 여성 분이 너의 이모니? (lady, standing, aunt, who)

_____

8   그는 다리가 한 개만 있는 이상한 의자를 발명했다. (invent, strange, have, only)

_____

9   나는 그녀의 집이 정말 예쁜 Amy를 나의 생일파티에 초대했다. (to, whose)

_____

10   그녀는 색깔이 분홍색인 드레스를 입고 파티에 나타났다. (show up, wearing, whose)

_____

Actual Test

다음 괄호 안의 주어진 단어를 이용하여 문장을 완성하세요.

1 내가 지금 정말 하고 싶은 것은 차가운 콜라를 마시는 것이다. (what, drinking, Coke)

_____

2 이것은 나의 삼촌이 개발한 어플리케이션이다. (application, develop, which)

_____

3 스마트폰을 바라보고 있던 그 소년은 작은 웅덩이를 디뎠다. (stare, step, in, puddle)

_____

4 돈만을 추구하는 그 사람들은 돈 때문에 실패할 수도 있다. (chase, only, may, because of)

_____

5 냄새가 아주 좋은 이 스파게티는 우리 엄마가 요리하셨다. (cooked by, whose, spaghetti)

_____

6 너희들이 지난주에 한 일은 매우 실망스러웠다. (what, disappointing)

_____

7 이것은 그 교수님으로부터 A등급을 받은 유일한 프로젝트이다. (the only, on, professor)

_____

8 이 모든 발명품은 아이큐(IQ)가 154인 Steve에 의해 발명되었다. (inventions, whose, invented)

_____

9 나는 몇몇의 스파이들을 보았고, 그들은 순식간에 사라졌다. (see, several, in an instant, who)

_____

10 아트 공원(Art Park)에는 그 캠페인에 참여했던 많은 소녀와 고양이들이 있었다. (campaign, there, take part in)

_____

New Words

novelist 소설가 | fall in love with ~와 사랑에 빠지다 | effectively 효과적으로 | employer 고용주, 사장 | employee 고용인, 직원 | hire 고용하다 | admire 존경하다 | compose 작곡하다 | aggressive 공격적인 | terrific 아주 멋진, 훌륭한 | irrevocable 돌이킬 수 없는 | show up 나타나다 | application 어플리케이션, 응용프로그램 | chase (돈 등을) 좇다, 추구하다 | puddle 웅덩이 | disappointing 실망스러운 | in an instant 순식간에 | take part in ~에 참여하다

UNIT 06 · 관계부사

A **관계부사의 종류** : 관계부사는 시간, 장소, 이유, 방법을 뜻하는 선행사를 수식하는 형용사절을 이끈다.

when (시간)	It's the time **when** children want to eat some snacks. 아이들이 과자를 먹기를 원하는 그 시간이다.
where (장소)	Many people like the country **where** there is no war. 많은 사람들은 전쟁이 없는 나라를 좋아한다.
why (이유)	This is the original reason **why** she left her country. 이것이 그녀가 그녀의 나라를 떠난 원래의 이유다.
how (방법)	I want to know **how** you completed this difficult task. = I want to know **the way** you completed this difficult task. 난 네가 이 어려운 업무를 완료한 방법을 알기를 원한다. 📝 관계부사 how는 선행사 the way와 함께 쓸 수 없다. 둘 중 하나만 써야 한다.

the time when children want to eat some snacks

B **관계부사의 생략** : 선행사나 관계부사 중 하나를 생략해서 쓸 수 있다.

I don't know **the reason why** Sophia loves you. 나는 Sophia가 너를 사랑하는 이유를 모르겠다.
= I don't know **the reason** Sophia loves you.
= I don't know **why** Sophia loves you.
📌 the time, the place, the reason처럼 일반적인 시간, 장소, 이유의 선행사는 주로 생략한다.

C **관계부사의 다른 표현들** : 「전치사 + 관계대명사」, / 「관계대명사 ~ 전치사」로 관계부사를 나타낼 수 있다.

I remember **the day when** you first called my name. 나는 네가 내 이름을 처음 불렀을 때를 기억한다.
= I remember **the day on which** you first called my name.
= I remember **the day which** you first called my name **on**.
= I remember the day **that** you first called my name **(on)**.
📌 관계부사 대신에 that을 쓸 수 있다. 단, 선행사를 생략하고 that을 쓸 수 없다.

 다음 중 어법에 맞는 것을 고르시오.

1 나는 그녀가 그 기계를 고쳤던 방법을 알고 싶다.
→ I want to know (the way how / the way) she fixed the machine.

2 나는 우리 가족이 처음으로 외식한 날을 기억한다.
→ I remember (the day that / that) my family ate out for the first time.

3 우리는 그가 왜 그 문을 열지 않았는지 모른다.
→ We don't know the reason (for which / which) he didn't open the door.

4 너는 Romeo와 Juliet이 태어난 장소를 알고 있니?
→ Do you know (the place / the way) where Romeo and Juliet were born?

Practice Test

다음 괄호 안의 주어진 단어를 이용하여 문장을 완성하세요.

1 이곳은 나의 아버지가 일하시는 은행이다. (this, where)

_____

2 오늘은 부모님이 20년 전에 결혼하셨던 그 날이다. (get married, when)

_____

3 Tony가 우유를 마시지 않는 이유를 나에게 말해줘. (reason)

_____

4 이것이 내가 사는 방식이다. (the way, live)

_____

5 그는 그녀와 듀엣으로 노래를 불렀던 그 무대를 기억했다. (sing a duet, the stage, where)

_____

6 밸런타인데이(Valentine's Day)는 여자들이 남자들에게 초콜릿을 주는 날이다. (chocolate, day)

_____

7 우리가 여름방학 휴가를 보내기 위해 가는 곳은 평화로워야 한다. (place, have a summer vacation, should)

_____

8 너희들이 다음 주에 거기에 갈 이유가 없다. (there, no reason why)

_____

9 우리는 내가 태어난 그 날에 결혼식을 올릴 것이다. (have a wedding, the day)

_____

10 그 선생님은 우리에게 어떻게 이 프로젝트가 성공했는지 설명해 주셨다. (explain, to, how)

_____

Actual Test ☆☆

What's your score? O 개 X 개

다음 괄호 안의 주어진 단어를 이용하여 문장을 완성하세요.

1 그것이 내가 그 강아지를 마지막으로 본 시간이었다. (it, the last time, when)

_____

2 이곳은 많은 미식가들이 밥을 먹는 유명한 식당이다. (gourmet, eat, restaurant, where)

_____

3 그녀는 그녀가 자신의 멘토를 만났던 그 날을 기억했다. (the day, when, mentor)

_____

4 이곳은 우리 할아버지가 태어나신 그 마을이다. (the town, here, where, born)

_____

5 야식을 먹는 것이 그가 조금도 살을 뺄 수 없는 이유다. (have a late-night meal, lose any weight)

_____

6 그는 자신이 맛있는 빵을 굽는 방식을 다른 사람과 공유하지 않는다. (the way, bake, share, delicious)

_____

7 스마트폰은 사람들이 외국에 있는 친구들과 쉽게 소통할 수 있는 방법이다. (abroad, interact, the way)

_____

8 많은 사람들이 성공할 수 없는 이유는 그들이 변화를 두려워하기 때문이다. (the reason, afraid of, that)

_____

9 그 초보운전자는 어떻게 그가 그때 깜빡이를 켰는지 기억할 수 없었다.
(novice driver, how, turn on the blinkers, at)

_____

10 8월 15일은 대한민국이 독립한 날이다. (the day, become, independent, when)

_____

New Words

original 원래의 ｜ eat out 외식하다 ｜ have a wedding 결혼식을 치르다[올리다] ｜ gourmet 미식가 ｜ mentor 멘토, 조언자 ｜
late-night meal 야식 ｜ lose weight 살이 빠지다 ｜ bake (빵 등을) 굽다 ｜ share 공유하다 ｜ interact with ~와 소통하다 ｜
novice 초보자 ｜ turn on the blinkers (자동차) 깜빡이를 켜다 ｜ independent 독립된

Correcting Errors ⭐Ⅰ

What's your score? O 개 X 개

다음 우리말과 같은 뜻이 되도록 어색한 부분을 바르게 고쳐 문장을 다시 쓰시오.

1 I remember the boy who mother is a famous writer.

→ _____

나는 엄마가 유명한 작가인 그 소년을 기억한다.

2 Please tell us that you saw last night.

→ _____

어젯밤에 당신이 본 것을 우리에게 말해 주세요.

3 Is there anything which interests you lately?

→ _____

최근에 너를 흥미롭게 하는 어떤 것이 있니?

4 The man has many cars, that are very expensive.

→ _____

그 남자는 많은 차들을 가지고 있는데, 그것들은 매우 비싸다.

5 She knows the way how she can pass the exam.

→ _____

그녀는 그 시험에 합격할 수 있는 방법을 안다.

6 Can you remember the restaurant when we had a great dinner together?

→ _____

너는 우리가 함께 근사한 저녁을 먹었던 그 식당을 기억할 수 있니?

7 Let's go to the zoo when we had a wonderful time.

→ _____

우리가 아주 멋진 시간을 보냈던 그 동물원으로 가자.

8 That I want to have now is comfortable shoes to run a marathon.

→ _____

내가 지금 가지고 싶은 것은 마라톤을 뛰기 위한 편안한 신발이다.

Correcting Errors II

작성일자 : _____월 _____일

다음 글에서 잘못된 부분을 올바르게 고쳐 전체 글을 다시 쓰시오.

My Childhood Friend

1 I visited somewhere quiet and beautiful last Saturday. The place I visited was my hometown. The reason how I visited there is to remember my childhood.

2 I met an old man who son's name is Jiseok. He was one of my friends when I was young.

3 I remember many times which I played with Jiseok. We lost contact after I moved to Seoul. I asked the old man the way how I could get in touch with Jiseok. He gave me Jiseok's cell phone number.

4 Tomorrow, I will call Jiseok, that was my good friend when I was young.

My Childhood Friend

1

2

3

4

New Words

visit 방문하다 | somewhere 어딘가에 | hometown 고향 | reason 이유 | childhood 어린 시절 | son 아들 | lose contact 연락이 끊어지다 | get [keep] in touch with ~와 연락하다 | call 전화하다

Paragraph Writing

작성일자 : _____ 월 _____ 일

필요한 부분에 관계대명사, 관계부사를 적절히 사용하여 다음 글을 영작하세요.

흰색 강아지

1 지난주에, 색깔이 하얀 귀여운 강아지 한 마리가 우리 집으로 들어왔다. 초등학생인 내 여동생은 나에게 그 강아지를 집에서 키우자고 말했다.

2 우리 집은 애완동물들이 생활할 수 없는 장소이다. 우리 집에 애완동물이 없는 이유는 우리 아빠가 동물을 좋아하지 않기 때문이다. 아빠가 동물들을 싫어하는 이유는 그가 어릴 적에 사나운 개에게 물렸던 적이 있기 때문이다.

3 그가 그 개에 물렸을 그때는 개를 키우는 데 있어서 지금과 달랐다. 대부분 사람들은 앞마당에서 개를 키웠다. 그러나 요즘에는 사람들이 집 안에서 개를 키운다. 나와 내 여동생은 아빠와 함께 동물 보호소에 가기로 했다. 그것이 그가 동물에 관심을 갖게 하는 유일한 방법일지도 모른다.

4 동물 보호소를 방문한 후 내가 우리 아빠에게 원하는 것은 그가 우리에게 그 흰색 개를 키우라고 허락하는 것이다.

A White Dog

Help!

be supposed to ~하기로 하다 | animal shelter 동물 보호소 | get interested in ~에 관심을 가지게 되다 | bitten bite(물다)의 과거분사 bite-bit-bitten | fierce 사나운 | for raising dogs 개를 키우는데 있어서 | front yard 앞마당 | allow A to B A가 B하는 것을 허락하다 | pet 애완동물

38

Chapter

4

to부정사와
동명사

to부정사와 동명사의 쓰임 ① 주어, 보어

A 주어로 쓰이는 to부정사

1 3인칭 단수로 취급한다.

<u>To protect my family</u> is necessary. 가족을 보호하는 것은 당연하다.
　　주어(S)　　　　　동사(V)

2 to부정사의 의미상 주어

· 「for + 목적격」: 문장의 주어와 동일하지 않을 경우

It is necessary **for me** to protect my family. 가족을 보호하는 것은 당연하다.
가주어　　　　　　의미상 주어　　　진주어

· 「of + 목적격」: 사람의 성품, 성격, 성질을 나타내는 형용사가 있을 경우

It is very generous **of him** to encourage the disappointed children.
가주어　　　　　　　의미상 주어　　　　　　진주어

실망한 아이들을 격려하는 것을 보니 그는 매우 관대하다.

사람의 성품은 of!

머래니?

사람 성품은 of래

B 주어로 쓰이는 동명사

1 3인칭 단수로 취급한다.

<u>Remembering new customers' names</u> is very important. 새로운 소비자들의 이름을 기억하는 것은 매우 중요하다.
　　　　주어(S)　　　　　　　동사(V)

2 동명사의 의미상 주어 : 주로 소유격을 쓴다. 📌 무생물 주어일 때는 목적격을 쓰기도 한다.

His **visiting** us made us excited. 그가 우리를 방문하는 것은 우리를 신나게 했다.

C 보어로 쓰이는 to부정사와 동명사

His final decision was **to support them** for two years. 그의 최종 결정은 2년 동안 그들을 지원하는 것이었다.
　　주어(S)　　　　　동사(V)　　보어(C)

What I do every day for my kids is **blessing them**. 내가 아이들을 위해 매일 하는 것은 그들의 축복을 빌어주는 것이다.
　　　　주어(S)　　　　　　　　동사(V)　　보어(C)

📌 to부정사와 동명사의 부정형은 not [never] to 동사원형 / not [never] 동사원형-ing이다.

Simple Test

다음 중 어법에 맞는 것을 고르시오.

1 우리 자신을 표현하는 것은 전혀 쉽지 않다.
→ (To express / Express) ourselves is not easy at all.

2 그가 그 환자를 오랫동안 돕는 것을 보니 매우 친절하다.
→ It is very kind (for / of) him to help the patient for a long time.

3 그 화가가 그녀의 초상화를 그리는 것은 매우 간단했다.
→ It was very simple (for / of) the painter to draw her portrait.

4 오늘의 업무는 100개의 이메일을 보내는 것이다.
→ Today's task is (send / sending) one hundred emails.

Practice Test

What's your score? O   개   X   개

다음 괄호 안의 주어진 단어를 이용하여 문장을 완성하세요.

1   무언가를 제시간에 시작하는 것은 매우 중요하다. (beginning, on time)

_____

2   너의 임무는 하루에 열 대의 차를 세차하는 것이다. (duty, to, wash, a day)

_____

3   우리 형의 꿈은 훌륭한 의사가 되는 것이다. (older, being, great)

_____

4   새로운 정보를 배우는 것은 너의 지식을 넓히는 것이다. (to learn, to broaden, knowledge)

_____

5   창문을 깨다니 그 소년은 매우 부주의했구나. (it, careless, to)

_____

6   이민자들이 문화 충격을 경험하는 것은 당연하다. (it, natural, immigrant, culture shock)

_____

7   그녀에게 꽃 백 송이를 사 주는 것은 그녀를 행복하게 할 것이다. (buying, will, make)

_____

8   수업 시간에 손을 드는 것은 너로 하여금 두려움을 극복하게 할 것이다. (raising, will, make, fear, overcome)

_____

9   그 강아지들에게 물을 주지 않는 것은 매우 잔인하다. (not, giving, to, cruel)

_____

10   많은 사람들 앞에서 그녀를 보호하는 것을 보니 그는 매우 용감하다. (it, brave, him, protect)

_____

Actual Test ☆☆

정답 p.09

What's your score? O   개 X   개

다음 괄호 안의 주어진 단어를 이용하여 문장을 완성하세요.

1 오랫동안 인내하는 것이 더 좋은 결과를 만들어낼 수 있다. (be, patient, create)

_____

2 너는 그들이 지난주에 서울(Seoul)로 돌아왔다는 소식을 들었니? (about, come, their)

_____

3 나는 그가 어제 우리 부모님을 방문한 것에 대해 정말 고맙게 생각한다. (appreciate, visiting)

_____

4 그 버릇없는 어린이들이 나를 따라오는 것은 매우 성가시다. (it, annoying, naughty)

_____

5 애국자들을 기억하는 것은 그들의 역사를 사람들에게 가르치는 데 있어 매우 중요하다.
(remembering, patriots, about)

_____

6 오늘의 매우 중요한 임무는 조난된 선원들을 빠르게 구조하는 것이다. (duty, shipwrecked, to rescue)

_____

7 그녀가 이번 주말에 할 수 없는 일은 가족 모임에 참석하는 것이다. (what, cannot, attend the family gathering)

_____

8 그녀의 약점을 모든 사람에게 말하지 않는 것을 보니 그는 매우 친절하다. (it, to tell, weak point)

_____

9 아이들이 매일 견과류를 먹는 것은 두뇌 발달에 효과적이다. (it, effective, nuts, every, for, development)

_____

10 그 타오르는 불길 속에서 그 아이를 데리고 나오는 것을 보니 그는 매우 용감하다.
(it, bring, child, to, out of, raging fire)

_____

New Words

generous 관대한 | task 업무 | duty 의무, 임무 | weak point 약점 | development 발달 | patriot 애국자 | rescue 구조하다 | shipwrecked 난파한, 조난당한 | attend 참석하다 | gathering 모임 | raging 타오르는 | appreciate 고맙게 여기다 | annoying 성가신, 귀찮은 | naughty 버릇없는 | follow 따라오다[가다] | sailor 선원 | effective 효과적인

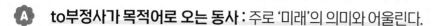

UNIT 08 to부정사와 동명사의 쓰임 ② 목적어

A to부정사가 목적어로 오는 동사 : 주로 '미래'의 의미와 어울린다.

want		expect	
hope		promise	
plan	to 동사원형	need	to 동사원형
decide		prepare	
agree		choose	

I **decided to** stay here for a week. 나는 일주일 동안 여기 머물기로 결심했다.
In my free time, I really **want to** get more rest at home. 여가 시간에, 나는 정말 집에서 더 쉬고 싶다.

B 동명사(-ing)가 목적어로 오는 동사 : 주로 '현재나 과거'의 의미와 어울린다.

enjoy		give up	
mind		quit	
finish	-ing	admit	-ing
avoid		put off	
deny		(= postpone, delay)	

Would you **mind opening** the window for a while? 잠시 창문을 열어도 될까요?
He **enjoys playing** tennis on weekends. 그는 주말마다 테니스 치는 것을 즐긴다.

Would you mind opening the window?

아이고 냄새

C to부정사와 동명사가 모두 목적어로 오는 동사

1 to부정사와 동명사가 목적어일 때 의미가 같은 동사 : like, love, hate, start, begin, continue 등
She likes **to eat (= eating)** spicy food. 그녀는 매운 음식을 먹는 것을 좋아한다.

2 to부정사와 동명사가 목적어일 때 의미가 다른 동사

to부정사	'미래'의 의미	동명사	'과거'의 의미
remember to 동사원형	~할 것을 기억하다	remember -ing	~했던 것을 기억하다
forget to 동사원형	~할 것을 잊어버리다	forget -ing	~했던 것을 잊어버리다
try to 동사원형	~하려고 노력하다	try -ing	시험 삼아 ~해보다
stop to 동사원형	~하기 위해 멈추다	stop -ing	~하는 것을 멈추다

Simple Test

다음 중 어법에 맞는 것을 고르시오.

1 그녀는 기말고사에 합격하기를 희망했다. → She hoped (to pass / passing) the final test.

2 그 소년은 모래성 만들기를 끝냈다. → The boy finished (to make / making) a sand castle.

3 Sam은 건강을 위해 너무 많은 고기를 먹는 것을 멈췄다.
→ Sam stopped (to eat / eating) too much meat for his health.

Practice Test

정답 p.09

What's your score? O   개 X   개

다음 괄호 안의 주어진 단어를 이용하여 문장을 완성하세요.

1   저 작은 고양이는 큰 생선을 먹고 싶어했다. (that, fish)

_____

2   그는 주말마다 골프 치는 것을 즐긴다. (every, golf, on)

_____

3   그녀는 오늘 오후에 박물관에 가는 것을 기억했다. (museum, this)

_____

4   그 평론가들은 마침내 서로 논쟁하는 것을 멈췄다. (critics, finally, argue)

_____

5   그 장거리 달리기 선수는 마라톤 풀코스 완주를 포기하지 않았다. (long distant runner, the full marathon)

_____

6   많은 고등학생들이 하루에 2시간 이상 수학을 공부하는 것을 싫어한다. (hate, many, studying, over)

_____

7   그녀는 신선한 과일들을 사기 위해 식료품 가게 앞에서 멈췄다. (grocery store)

_____

8   학생들은 학교 와이파이(Wi-Fi)의 비밀번호를 계속 찾았다. (continue, find out, of)

_____

9   Jack은 작년에 많은 돈을 기부했던 것을 잊어버렸다. (forget, donate)

_____

10   내가 그의 제안을 받아들이는 것을 거부해야 하니? (have to, deny, accept, proposal)

_____

Actual Test

정답 p.10

What's your score? O   개 X   개

다음 괄호 안의 주어진 단어를 이용하여 문장을 완성하세요.

1   제 가방을 당신의 사무실에 잠시 두어도 될까요? (would, mind, put, while)

_____

2   엄마는 가스레인지를 끄는 것을 자주 잊어버리신다. (forget, gas stove, often)

_____

3   그 쥐는 고양이를 피하기 위해 작은 구멍을 찾으려고 노력했다. (avoid, try, hole)

_____

4   나는 작년에 고향 친구들과 즐거운 시간을 보냈던 것을 기억한다. (hometown, have a good time)

_____

5   그 어린이들은 공포 영화를 보는 것을 피했다. (avoid, watch, horror movies)

_____

6   그녀는 대중들이 그녀의 사생활에 관해 알게 되는 것을 꺼렸다. (mind, have, the public, private)

_____

7   우리는 폭풍 때문에 서둘러서 그 도시를 떠날 필요가 있었다. (need, because of, storm, in a hurry)

_____

8   나의 조부모님은 시골에서 옛 친구들과 함께 사는 것을 즐기신다. (live in the country)

_____

9   소파 위에서, 그녀는 노트북으로 이메일을 보내는 것을 끝냈다. (finish, with her laptop computer)

_____

10   그들은 다음 달에 큰 회의를 개최하는 것을 갑자기 연기했다. (conference, hold, suddenly delayed)

_____

New Words

deny 부인하다 | critic 평론가 | argue 논쟁을 벌이다, 말다툼하다 | long distance runner 장거리 주자 | give up 포기하다 |
finish the full marathon 마라톤 풀코스를 완주하다 | accept 받아들이다 | proposal 제안 | gas stove 가스레인지 | avoid 피하다 |
dishonest 부정직한 | private 개인적인, 사적인 | storm 폭풍 | in a hurry 서둘러서 | hold 개최하다

Correcting Errors ⓘ

정답 p.10

What's your score? O 개 X 개

다음 우리말과 같은 뜻이 되도록 어색한 부분을 바르게 고쳐 문장을 다시 쓰시오.

1 Can you finish to make the cake in two hours?

→ _____

너는 두 시간 후에 그 케이크를 만드는 것을 끝낼 수 있니?

2 To solve these problems are not easy for me.

→ _____

이 문제들을 해결하는 것은 나에게 쉽지 않다.

3 Today's duty is to feeding the fish in the aquarium.

→ _____

오늘의 임무는 수족관에 있는 물고기에게 먹이를 주는 것이다.

4 Don't give up to memorize the numbers even if it seems difficult.

→ _____

어려운 것처럼 보일지라도 그 숫자들을 외우는 것을 포기하지 마.

5 She'll never forget to travel across Europe.

→ _____

그녀는 유럽 전역을 여행했던 것을 결코 잊지 않을 것이다.

6 You have to stop to eat fast food for your health.

→ _____

너는 너의 건강을 위해 패스트푸드를 먹는 것을 그만둬야 한다.

7 They really wanted experiencing the joy of adventure.

→ _____

그들은 정말 모험의 즐거움을 경험하고 싶었다.

8 It is very nice for her to help the children.

→ _____

그 아이들을 돕는 걸 보니 그녀는 매우 착하다.

Correcting Errors ⅠⅠ

작성일자 : _____월 _____일

다음 글에서 잘못된 부분을 올바르게 고쳐 전체 글을 다시 쓰시오.

Playing Badminton

1 Play badminton is very good for your health. I play it every Sunday.

2 My father is one of my best friends. He helps me to play it well. It is very nice for him to help me.

3 I remember to learn badminton for the first time when I was 8 years old. We enjoyed to play it together. I was poor at playing it, but my father didn't give up to teach me. Thanks to my father, I learned playing it very well. Be healthy is very important. I am trying to lose weight by playing badminton.

4 Now, I am very good at playing badminton. Do you want playing badminton with me? You will be much healthier if you play badminton.

Playing Badminton

1

2

3

4

New Words

health 건강 | learn 배우다 | together 함께, 같이 | be poor at ~에 서투르다, ~을 못하다 | give up 포기하다 | teach 가르치다 | thanks to ~덕분에, ~때문에 | be good at ~에 능숙하다, ~을 잘하다

Paragraph Writing

작성일자 : _____월 _____일

필요한 부분에 to부정사와 동명사를 적절히 사용하여 다음 글을 영작하세요.

스피너

1 학생들은 때때로 스피너를 가지고 노는 것을 좋아한다. 내 남동생도 스피너를 가지고 노는 것을 즐긴다.

2 누가 스피너를 발명했는지 나는 모르지만, 많은 학생들은 그들이 스피너를 돌릴 때 편안함을 느낀다고 말한다. 스피너가 사용되는 이유는 공부에 지친 학생들이 긴장을 푸는 방법으로 스피너를 선택하기 때문일 수 있다.

3 스피너를 돌리는 것은 너무 재미있다. 내가 어렸을 때 바람개비를 가지고 놀았던 것을 기억한다. 스피너는 그냥 바람개비 같은 것이라고 생각한다. 스피너와 바람개비는 꾸준하게 돌아간다.

4 인생도 끊임없이 돌아가는 스피너와 같다. 내 미래의 꿈을 잃어버리지 않기 위해 나는 내일도 최선을 다하고 싶다.

Spinners

Help!

spinner 스피너 | be bored with (= be tired of) ~에 지친 | relax 쉬게 하다, 긴장을 풀다 | spin 돌리다 | pinwheel 바람개비 | steadily 꾸준하게 | constantly 끊임없이

Chapter

5

완료시제

UNIT 09 현재완료와 과거

A **현재완료** : 과거의 어느 한 시점부터 현재까지 영향을 미치는 것을 나타내기 위한 표현

1 현재완료 「have [has] + p.p.」 용법

완료	막 ~했다	just, already, still, yet 등과 주로 함께 쓴다.
		He **has just finished** his task. 그는 막 그의 업무를 마쳤다.
결과	~했다, 그 결과 ~인 상태이다	과거의 결과가 현재에도 영향을 미친다.
		He **has lost** his cell phone. 그는 그의 휴대전화를 잃어버렸다. (지금도 잃어버린 상태)
경험	~한 적이 있다	before, ever, never, once, twice, times와 주로 함께 쓴다.
		I **have been to** Africa before. 나는 전에 아프리카에 간 적이 있다.
계속	계속 ~해왔다	always, since, for 등과 주로 함께 쓴다.
		She **has studied** Spanish since 2022. 그녀는 2022년 이후로 스페인어를 공부해 왔다.

📌 have been과 have gone의 차이
> ex I have been to Japan. 나는 일본에 가본 적이 있다. (갔다가 옴) / He has gone to Japan. 그는 일본에 갔다. (가버리고 없음)

2 현재완료는 과거의 한 시점을 나타내는 시간 표현과 함께 쓸 수 없다.

I have finished my homework this morning. (×)

→ I **finished** my homework **this morning**. (O) 나는 오늘 아침 숙제를 끝냈다.

📌 현재완료는 특정 시점을 묻는 when과 함께 쓸 수 없다.
> ex When have you met him? (x) / When did you meet him? (o) 너는 언제 그를 만났니?

B **과거 시제** : 명확한 과거를 나타내고 싶을 때 📌 yesterday, last, age 등과 함께 쓴다.

He **visited** his grandparents last week. 그는 지난주에 조부모님을 방문했다.

C **현재완료 진행형** : have [has] been –ing '(계속) ~해오고 있는 중이다, ~해오고 있다'

They **have been selling** special pizza. 그들은 특별한 피자를 계속 팔고 있다.

Simple Test

다음 중 어법에 맞는 것을 고르시오.

1 그는 브라질에 두 번 가본 적 있다.
→ He (has been / has gone) to Brazil twice.

2 그들은 작년에 보스턴을 방문했다.
→ They (have visited / visited) Boston last year.

3 너는 인도 음식을 전에 먹어본 적 있니?
→ (Have you eaten / Did you eat) Indian food before?

4 그는 3시간 동안 그 기계를 고치고 있는 중이다.
→ He has been (repairing / repaired) the machine for three hours.

Practice Test

What's your score? O 　개 X 　개

현재완료 또는 현재완료 진행형을 사용해서 다음 우리말을 영작하세요.

1 그들은 벌써 서울(Seoul)에 도착했다. (arrive, already)

_____

2 너는 제주도(Jeju Island)에서 살아본 적 있니? (ever)

_____

3 너는 그를 오랫동안 알고 지냈니? (known, for a long time)

_____

4 그는 아직 집으로 돌아오지 않았다. (yet, come)

_____

5 그 화가는 그의 초상화를 그리는 것을 막 끝냈다. (just, paint, finish, portrait)

_____

6 그 엔지니어들은 열심히 일해오고 있는 중이다. (engineers, working)

_____

7 너는 대구(Daegu)에 산 지 얼마나 됐어? (how long)

_____

8 그 소년들은 단 한 번도 그 건물에 간 적이 없다. (never, to the building)

_____

9 그녀는 하루 종일 택배 기사를 기다리고 있는 중이다. (delivery man, all day long)

_____

10 그들은 10년 동안 그의 인생 이야기를 들어왔다. (hear, life story, for)

_____

Actual Test

정답 p.11

What's your score? O ___ 개 X ___ 개

현재완료 또는 현재완료 진행형을 사용해서 다음 우리말을 영작하세요.

1 Jaden은 어릴 때부터 그의 할머니 집에 살았다. (live, at)

_____

2 Beth는 아프리카(Africa)에 두 번 가본 적 있다. (twice)

_____

3 우리는 아직도 우리의 과제를 끝내지 못했다. (assignment, finish, yet)

_____

4 너는 언제 그 대회에 참석했니? (take part in, when, contest)

_____

5 우리는 10년 넘게 서로에게 좋은 친구였다. (for, over, good)

_____

6 나의 형은 또 다른 오디션을 위해 이미 서울(Seoul)로 떠났다. (leave for, already, for, audition)

_____

7 그 광부들은 그 광산에서 5시간 동안 석탄을 캐고 있는 중이다. (miner, mine, coal)

_____

8 우리는 우리의 휴가를 위해 돈을 저금해오고 있지 않았다. (save, vacation)

_____

9 너는 다른 나라에서 문화 충격을 경험한 적이 있니? (culture shock, another)

_____

10 일부 정치인들은 뇌물을 받아서 자신들의 양심을 내버렸다.
(some, politician, throw away, conscience, take bribes)

_____

New Words

task 업무 | twice 두 번 | Indian 인도의 | portrait 초상화 | delivery man 택배 기사 | life story 인생 이야기 | mine 광산; 채굴하다 | miner 광부 | coal 석탄 | assignment 과제 | defend 방어하다 | culture shock 문화 충격 | resident 주민 | save 저금하다 | politician 정치인 | conscience 양심 | throw away (내)버리다 | take bribes 뇌물을 받다

UNIT 10 과거완료와 미래완료

A 과거완료 「had + p.p.」

1 쓰임 : 대과거(더 오래된 과거)에서 과거 어느 시점까지 일어난 일을 표현한다.

2 과거완료 용법

완료	He **had just finished** his homework. 그는 막 그의 숙제를 마쳤(었)다.
결과	She **had lost** her ring. 그녀는 그녀의 반지를 잃어버렸(었)다.
경험	She **had never eaten** meat. 그녀는 고기를 먹은 적이 전혀 없었다.
계속	I **had tried** to change my bad habit. 나는 내 나쁜 습관을 바꾸려고 노력해 왔(었)다.

3 과거형과 과거완료의 비교

She **had already left** the station when the train **arrived**.
기차가 도착했을 때, 그녀는 이미 역을 떠났(었)다.

📌 시간 순서에 따른 표현에 유의하자. (그녀가 떠나고 난 후에 기차가 도착했음)

가지마!
No! No! No!

B 미래완료 「will have + p.p.」

1 쓰임 : 현재로부터 시작해서 미래의 한 시점까지 연결되는 일을 표현한다.

2 해석 : '~한 셈이 된다, ~일 것이다, ~하게 될 것이다'

3 when, if, by, by the time, before, after와 주로 함께 쓴다.

4 미래완료 용법 📌 시간과 조건의 부사절은 주절에 미래완료 시제가 와도 종속절에는 현재시제를 사용한다.

완료	I **will have finished** my homework by tomorrow. 내일까지 나는 숙제를 끝낼 것이다.
결과	They **will have left** when I get there. 내가 그곳에 도착한 때에 그들은 떠나고 없을 것이다.
경험	I **will have read** this novel three times if I read it again. 내가 만약 그 소설을 한 번 더 읽는다면 세 번 읽는 셈이 된다.
계속	We **will have lived** here for 20 years by next year. 내년이면 우리는 여기 20년 동안 산 셈이 된다.

Simple Test

다음 중 어법에 맞는 것을 고르시오.

1 나는 내일이면 거기에 도착했을 것이다.
→ I (have arrived / will have arrived) there by tomorrow.

2 그가 그곳에 도착했을 때 그 가게는 닫혀 있었다.
→ The store (closed / had closed) when he got there.

3 내가 한 번 더 그곳에 가면 제주도에 다섯 번 가는 셈이 된다.
→ I (will be / will have been) to Jeju Island five times if I go there one more time.

4 그녀가 또 다른 선물을 보낸다면 두 개의 선물을 보낸 셈이 된다.
→ She will have sent two presents if she (sends / will send) another present.

Practice Test

What's your score? O   개   X   개

과거완료 또는 미래완료를 사용해서 다음 우리말을 영작하세요.

1   그 사슴은 그때까지 살아 있었다. (alive, until, then)

_____

2   그는 전에 도쿄(Tokyo)에 가본 적이 있었다. (to, before)

_____

3   나는 그때까지는 외국인들과 영어로 한 번도 말한 적이 없었다. (speak, never, foreigners)

_____

4   나는 지난주에 산 나의 새 안경을 잃어버렸다. (glasses, which)

_____

5   그녀가 나에게 전화했을 때 난 이미 나의 보고서를 제출했었다. (submit, report)

_____

6   비가 내리기 전에 그는 이미 세차를 했다. (before, rain, already)

_____

7   내가 이메일을 보냈을 때 그는 이미 그의 사무실을 떠났었다. (leave, office)

_____

8   Sean이 캐나다(Canada)에 다시 간다면 그는 거기 다섯 번째 가는 셈이 된다. (if, been, there)

_____

9   다음 달이면 내가 1년 동안 이 식당을 운영한 셈이 된다. (by, run)

_____

10   네가 돌아올 때쯤이면 나는 너의 컴퓨터를 고쳤을 것이다. (by the time, fix)

_____

Actual Test

What's your score? O   개   X   개

과거완료 또는 미래완료를 사용해서 다음 우리말을 영작하세요.

1 그녀는 그가 이미 그 방을 청소했다고 나에게 말했다. (clean)

_____

2 구급차가 그곳에 도착했을 때 사람들은 이미 사라졌다. (ambulance, arrive, disappear)

_____

3 그 건설 노동자들은 내년까지 그 집을 철거하지 않을 것이다. (by, construction workers, demolish)

_____

4 내년이면 내가 서울에 산 지 20년이 되는 셈이다. (by, live)

_____

5 내가 부엌으로 갔을 때 우리 엄마는 이미 저녁 준비를 끝내셨다. (preparing dinner)

_____

6 그 부유한 상인이 돈을 보냈을 때 그녀는 이미 은행에 있었다. (merchant, at)

_____

7 Jina는 다음 주 일요일이면 병원에 입원한 지 두 달이 된다. (by, be in the hospital)

_____

8 그들이 그 콘서트장에 도착했을 때 표가 이미 다 팔렸었다. (concert hall, sold out)

_____

9 나의 조부모님은 내년이면 50년간 결혼 생활을 해 온 셈이 된다. (be, married, by)

_____

10 내가 집에 왔을 때 누군가가 나의 치킨을 벌써 다 먹었다. (come, eat, chicken)

_____

New Words

habit 습관 | alive 살아있는 | foreigner 외국인 | submit 제출하다 | run 경영하다, 운영하다 | fix 수리하다, 고치다 | ambulance 구급차 | disappear 사라지다 | demolish 철거하다 | construction worker 건설 노동자, 공사현장 인부 | merchant 상인 | be in (the) hospital 병원에 입원해 있다 | sell out 다 팔리다, 매진되다

Correcting Errors ⭐Ⅰ

다음 우리말과 같은 뜻이 되도록 어색한 부분을 바르게 고쳐 문장을 다시 쓰시오.

1 Jack has finished his project yesterday.

→ _____

Jack은 어제 그의 프로젝트를 끝냈다.

2 Have you ever been going to France?

→ _____

너는 프랑스에 가본 적 있니?

3 When his mom came back home, he has already cleaned his room.

→ _____

그의 엄마가 집에 돌아 왔을 때 그는 이미 그의 방을 청소했었다.

4 I have been living in Seoul for 15 years if I stay for one more month.

→ _____

내가 한 달 더 머무르면 나는 서울에서 15년 동안 산 셈이 된다.

5 When have you called Jane?

→ _____

너는 Jane에게 언제 전화했니?

6 They are waiting for the singer since morning.

→ _____

그들은 아침부터 그 가수를 기다려 오고 있는 중이다.

7 My younger brother has already removed the file when I entered the room.

→ _____

내가 그 방에 들어갔을 때 나의 남동생은 이미 그 파일을 삭제했었다.

8 If he goes again, he will had been Jeju Island three times.

→ _____

그가 다시 간다면 그는 제주도에 세 번 간 셈이 된다.

Correcting Errors II

다음 글에서 잘못된 부분을 올바르게 고쳐 전체 글을 다시 쓰시오.

Art Museum

1 I have visited an art museum with my friends yesterday. The art museum will have open for 20 years by next month.

2 The museum collects a lot of paintings before a new museum was needed. The city wants to collect even more paintings but this is too small.

3 Many people has asked the city to build a new art museum for a long time. So, the mayor of the city has just decided to build a new art museum.

4 The art museum has long opening hours and is free to the public. I had great time with my friends there.

Art Museum

1

2

3

4

New Words

art museum 미술관 | collect 모으다, 수집하다 | painting 그림 | mayor 시장 | decide ~을 결정하다 | free 무료의 | the public 일반 국민, 대중 | build 짓다, 건설하다 | opening hours 관람[영업] 시간

Paragraph Writing

작성일자 : _____ 월 _____ 일

필요한 부분에 현재완료, 과거, 과거완료, 미래완료를 적절히 사용하여 다음 글을 영작하세요.

해외여행

1 나는 한 번도 해외여행을 가본 적이 없다. 내 친구 Daniel이 그의 여행들에 대해 나에게 말해 주기 전에 나는 여행에 흥미가 없었다.

2 그는 일본과 중국에 딱 한 번 가본 적이 있고, 미국에는 두 번 가본 적이 있다. 그는 내년이면 유럽에 가 있을 것이다. 최근에 그는 나에게 여행에서 얻는 즐거움을 알게 해 주었다.

3 하지만, 그는 다음 여행을 위해서 돈을 조금 준비해야 한다고 나에게 말했다. 나는 Daniel 이 준비를 많이 해 왔다고 생각했다. 나는 5년 동안 은행에 많은 돈을 저축해왔다.

4 내년에는 나 혼자 여행을 가게 될 것이고, 내년 여름이면 나는 친구 Daniel과 유럽에서 즐거운 시간을 보내고 있을 것이다.

Traveling overseas

Help!

travel (먼 거리를) 여행하다 | overseas 해외로, 외국으로 | trip (특히 짧은) 여행 | Europe 유럽 | recently 최근에 |
get pleasure from ~에서 기쁨을 얻다 | prepare 준비하다 | save 저축하다 | have a good time 즐거운 시간을 보내다

Chapter

6

수동태

UNIT 11 단순형 수동태

아뿔싸!
그새 딱지가…

A 수동태란 무엇인가?

1 의미 : 주어가 직접 행하는 게 아니라 행해지거나 당하는 것

2 형태 : 「be동사 + p.p. + (by + 행위자)」 📌 「by +행위자」는 자주 생략된다.

Good people **are welcomed**. 착한 사람들은 환영 받는다.

B 여러 가지 수동태

1 4형식의 수동태 : 「주어(S) +동사(V) +간접목적어(IO) +직접목적어(DO)」를 수동태로 변형시킨 것

· 목적어(IO/DO) 중 하나를 문장의 주어로 보내고, 다른 하나는 그대로 두는 형태이다.

The policeman gave **her a fine** for parking illegally. 경찰은 그녀에게 불법 주차에 대한 벌금을 부과했다.

→ **She was given a fine** (by the policeman) for parking illegally. (간접목적어 주어)

→ **A fine was given (to) her** (by the policeman) for parking illegally. (직접목적어 주어)

2 5형식의 수동태 : 「주어(S) +동사(V) +목적어(O) +목적격 보어(OC)」를 수동태로 변형시킨 것

· 목적어(O)를 문장의 주어로 보내고, 목적격 보어(OC)는 그대로 두는 형태이다.

· 사역동사와 지각동사를 수동태로 만들 때 목적격 보어를 to부정사로 바꾼다.

He saw a boy **sing** in English. 그는 소년이 영어로 노래하는 것을 보았다.

→ A boy **was seen to sing** in English.

C by 이외의 전치사를 쓰는 수동태

be covered with	~로 덮여 있다	be known for	~로 유명하다
be filled with	~로 가득하다	be known as	~로 알려져 있다
be satisfied with	~에 만족하다	be known to	~에게 알려져 있다
be interested in	~에 흥미가 있다	be surprised at [by]	~에 놀라다
be engaged in	~에 종사하다	be caught in	(비, 폭풍 등)을 만나다

Many people **are engaged in** the IT field these days. 요즘음 많은 사람들이 IT분야에 종사한다.

Simple Test

다음 중 어법에 맞는 것을 고르시오.

1 그녀는 그 뉴스에 매우 놀랐다.

→ She was very surprised (at / in) the news.

2 그 고기는 냉동고에 얼려졌다.

→ The meat (froze / was frozen) in the freezer.

3 Fred는 그녀의 차를 세차하게 되었다.

→ Fred was made (washed / to wash) her car.

Practice Test

수동태를 사용해서 다음 우리말을 영작하세요.

1 그 교수는 Tim의 논문에 매우 만족해했다. (thesis, satisfied)

_____

2 그의 소설은 많은 사람들에게 알려져 있다. (novel, known)

_____

3 그 편지는 어제 스페인(Spain)으로 보내졌다. (send)

_____

4 영어는 많은 나라에서 사용된다. (speak, in)

_____

5 Max는 그의 할머니에 의해 길러졌다. (raise)

_____

6 그 걸작은 재능 있는 예술가에 의해 만들어졌다. (masterpiece, create, talented)

_____

7 그 소녀는 그녀의 등을 빠른 공에 의해 맞았다. (hit, on her back)

_____

8 그 고장 난 낡은 시계는 어제 수리되었다. (clock, break, repair)

_____

9 그 파리는 저 벌레 살충제에 의해 죽었다. (bug spray, kill)

_____

10 그 나이 든 남자는 산삼을 찾는 데 관심이 있었다. (old man, finding, wild ginseng)

_____

Actual Test

정답 p.13

What's your score? O ___ 개 X ___ 개

수동태를 사용해서 다음 우리말을 영작하세요.

1   이 오래된 도자기는 500년 전에 만들어졌다. (piece, pottery, make)

_____

2   그들은 집에 가는 길에 폭우를 만났다. (caught, heavy, on their way)

_____

3   그의 지저분한 방은 그의 누나에 의해 청소되었다. (messy, his sister, clean up)

_____

4   Molly의 엄마는 그녀에게 약간의 계란을 사도록 했다. (Molly를 주어로) (make, some eggs)

_____

5   많은 친구들이 Julia가 무대 위에서 기타를 치는 것을 보았다. (Julia를 주어로) (on the stage)

_____

6   나는 강 위에 아름다운 무지개가 떴다고 들었다. (told, that, rainbow, come out)

_____

7   많은 뉴스들이 거짓으로 쓰여졌다는 것은 충격적이다. (it, untruthfully, shocking)

_____

8   그 남자가 그 아이에게 초콜릿을 조금 주었다. (그 아이를 주어로) (chocolate)

_____

9   나의 영어 선생님은 나에게 하루에 10개의 단어를 외우라고 권했다. (나를 주어로)
     (advise, memorize, vocabulary words)

_____

10 그의 상사는 그 자동차 판매원에게 한 달에 열 대의 차를 팔게 했다. (그 자동차 판매원을 주어로)
     (the car salesman, make, sell)

_____

New Words

fine 벌금 | illegally 불법적으로 | frozen freeze(얼다)의 과거분사 | freezer 냉동고 | thesis 논문 | raise 양육하다 | masterpiece 걸작 | repair 수리하다 | bug spray 살충제 | wild ginseng 산삼 | pottery 도자기 | memorize 암기하다 | heavy rain 폭우 | messy 지저분한 | untruthfully 거짓으로 | car salesman 자동차 판매원

A 조동사의 수동태 : 「조동사 + be + p.p.」

Nothing **can be seen** here. 여기에는 아무 것도 안 보인다.

A big building **will be constructed** on this site. 큰 건물이 이 장소에 건설될 것이다.

B that절이 이끄는 문장의 수동태

「They say that 주어 + 동사」 : '사람들이 ~라고 말한다.'

= 「It is said that 주어 + 동사」 = 「주어 + is said to + 동사원형」

They say that knowledge is power. 사람들은 아는 것이 힘이라고 말한다.

= **It is said that** knowledge is power. = **Knowledge is said to** be power.

C 구동사의 수동태

He **took care of** his son alone for a long time. 그는 오랫동안 혼자서 그의 아들을 돌봤다.

= His son **was taken care of** by him alone for a long time.

📌 구동사란 단어 2개 이상의 덩어리로 이루어진 동사를 말한다. 구동사 전체를 하나의 덩어리로 보고 함께 움직인다.

D to부정사와 동명사의 수동태

1 to부정사의 수동태 : 「to + be + p.p.」

She wanted her room **to be cleaned** every day. 그녀는 그녀의 방이 매일 청소되길 원했다.

2 동명사의 수동태 : 「being + p.p.」

Nobody likes **being treated** like a slave. 아무도 노예처럼 대우받기를 좋아하지 않는다.

E 관용 표현

be supposed to 동사원형	~하기로 되어 있다	be required to 동사원형	~하도록 요구되다
be obliged to 동사원형	~해야 한다	be scheduled to 동사원형	~할 예정이다

Simple Test 다음 중 어법에 맞는 것을 고르시오.

1 우리는 이 콘서트가 연기되기를 원한다.

→ We want this concert (to delay / to be delayed).

2 사람들은 유기농 채소가 몸에 좋다고 말한다.

→ It (says / is said) that organic vegetables are good for health.

3 그 금고는 내일 그 지역 은행으로 보내질 것이다.

→ The safety deposit box (will send / will be sent) to the local bank tomorrow.

Practice Test

What's your score? O   개   X   개

수동태를 사용해서 다음 우리말을 영작하세요.

1 그는 주간 회의에 참석하라는 요구를 받다. (required, weekly, attend, to)

_____

2 어느 누구도 여기에 들어오는 것이 허락될 수 없다. (nobody, allow)

_____

3 그는 나에게 좀 더 자주 쉬라고 조언했다. (advise, relax, to)

_____

4 사람들은 양파가 몸에 좋다고 말한다. (onions를 주어로)

_____

5 그 아이는 용감한 남자에 의해 보호받고 있었다. (being, child, protect)

_____

6 그녀는 한 달에 한 번씩 건강 검진을 받아야 한다. (a medical check-up, obliged)

_____

7 그들은 James의 초대로 축제에 참여하였다. (축제를 주어로) (take part in, by them, because of)

_____

8 그녀는 최고의 글로벌 회사에 채용될 것이다. (recruit, will, top-ranked)

_____

9 그는 좋은 점수 덕분에 상을 받게 될 것이다. (given, prize, thanks to, good marks)

_____

10 사람들은 스마트폰이 의사소통에 좋지 않다고 말한다. (It을 주어로) (for, communication)

_____

Actual Test

정답 p.14

What's your score? O   개 X   개

수동태를 사용해서 다음 우리말을 영작하세요.

1 그 손님들은 오늘 저녁에 전통 식당을 방문할 예정이다. (scheduled, traditional restaurant)

_____

2 불필요한 파일들이 오늘 오후에 그 직원에 의해 제거되었다. (get rid of, unnecessary, the staff)

_____

3 그들의 바람은 신선한 음식을 제공 받는 것이었다. (desire, being, serve)

_____

4 우유가 불면증 극복에 좋다고들 말한다. (It을 주어로) (that, overcoming of insomnia)

_____

5 이 비행기는 홍콩(Hong Kong)에 도착하기로 되어 있었다. (suppose, arrive, airplane)

_____

6 다른 팀으로 이적되는 것은 운동선수들을 몹시 실망시킨다. (being, trade, athletes)

_____

7 사람들은 진정한 자유란 서로 사랑하는 것이라고 한다. (It을 주어로) (freedom, loving)

_____

8 사람들은 James가 항상 남을 배려한다고들 한다. (James를 주어로) (said, considerate of others, all the time)

_____

9 그 회사가 무언가를 숨기고 있다는 사실은 대중에게 알려져야 한다.
(the fact that, company, hide, should, known, public)

_____

10 우리는 그 중요 문서들이 가능한 빨리 그 변호사에게 보내지길 바란다.
(documents, hope, as, soon, possible, to, send)

_____

New Words

organic 유기농의 | safety deposit box 금고 | medical check-up 건강 검진 | invitation 초대 | top-ranked 최상위의 | recruit 채용하다 | get rid of ~을 제거하다 | overcome 극복하다 | insomnia 불면증 | considerate 배려하는

Correcting Errors Ⅰ

What's your score? O   개 X   개

다음 우리말과 같은 뜻이 되도록 어색한 부분을 바르게 고쳐 문장을 다시 쓰시오.

1 They were satisfied by the final score.

→ _____

그들은 그 최종 점수에 만족했다.

2 The patient was made take the medicine every day by the doctor.

→ _____

그 환자는 그 의사에 의해 매일 그 약을 복용하게 되었다.

3 He was interesting in collecting toy cars.

→ _____

그는 장난감 차들을 수집하는 것에 흥미가 있었다.

4 The report should submitted by tomorrow.

→ _____

그 보고서는 내일까지 제출되어야 한다.

5 This marble can be seeing in the dark because it glows.

→ _____

이 구슬은 빛나기 때문에 어둠 속에서도 보일 수 있다.

6 It is said to walnuts are good for the brains.

→ _____

사람들은 호두가 뇌에 좋다고들 말한다.

7 He wanted the packages to send to Canada.

→ _____

그는 그 소포들이 캐나다로 보내지는 것을 원했다.

8 Some trash was got(ten) from the street rid of.

→ _____

일부의 쓰레기가 거리에서부터 제거되어졌다.

Correcting Errors Ⅱ

작성일자 : _____월 _____일

다음 글에서 잘못된 부분을 올바르게 고쳐 전체 글을 다시 쓰시오.

The Importance of Preparation

1 I supposed to meet some potential new clients tomorrow. Being chose by new clients is very exciting.

2 It said that preparing well is very important to attracting people's attention.

3 I have a lot of things to prepare for tomorrow's meeting. I am interested at making a good presentation. An effective presentation will be show to the clients. There will be over five people who will compete for this business.

4 However, I am sure that my suggestions will selected. I want the clients to be satisfying. I think that preparing hard makes someone a winner. Why don't you prepare to win?

The Importance of Preparation

1

2

3

4

New Words

potential 가능성이 있는, 잠재적인 | client 고객, 의뢰인 | prepare for ~을 준비하다 | effective 효과적인 | presentation 발표(회) | suggestion 제안 | compete 경쟁하다, 경쟁을 벌이다 | select 선택하다 | satisfy 만족시키다

Paragraph Writing

작성일자 : _____ 월 _____ 일

필요한 부분에 수동태를 적절히 사용하여 다음 글을 영작하세요.

전쟁과 평화

1 어제 할아버지가 나에게 한국전쟁에 관해 이야기해 주셨다. 1950년, 어느 일요일 새벽에 남한은 갑자기 북한에 의해 공격을 당했고, 많은 사람들이 피난을 가야 했다.

2 몇몇 키가 큰 할아버지 친구들은 전투를 위해 급히 보내졌다. 할아버지는 키가 작으셔서 전투에 투입되지 않았다. 많은 할아버지의 친구들이 그 전쟁터에서 목숨을 잃었다. 끔찍한 일이었다.

전쟁이란 참혹하고 무서운 것이란다.

진지 진지

3 사람들은 전쟁이 다시 일어나도록 해서는 안 된다고 말한다. 나는 평화가 세계 곳곳으로 퍼져나가야 한다고 생각한다. 모든 사람들이 평화를 위해 연합되어야 한다.

4 그래서 나는 나의 친구들과 좋은 관계를 유지하려고 노력한다. 이는 평화를 향한 첫걸음이 될 것이다.

War and Peace

Help!

the Korean War 한국전쟁 | one Sunday at dawn 어느 일요일 새벽에 | attack 공격하다 | flee 달아나다, 도망하다 | battle 전쟁터 | terrible 끔찍한 | It is said that... ~라고 한다 | spread 퍼뜨리다, 보급시키다 | occur 일어나다, 발생하다 | unite 연합하다 | relationship 관계 | toward ~쪽으로, ~을 향하여

68

Chapter

7

분사

UNIT 13 현재분사와 과거분사

Ⓐ 현재분사와 과거분사

1 현재분사 : 「동사원형 + -ing」 '~하는, 하고 있는' (능동)

The **sleeping baby** is very cute. 잠자는 아기는 매우 귀엽다. (명사 수식)

They are **dancing** at the party. 그들은 파티에서 춤을 추고 있다. (진행형)

2 과거분사 : 동사의 과거분사 (p.p.) '~해진, ~된' (수동)

The **broken window** is very dangerous to children. 깨진 창문은 아이들에게 매우 위험하다. (명사 수식)

The deer was **caught** by the lion. 사슴이 사자에 의해 잡혔다. (수동태)

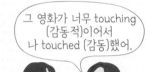

Ⓑ 감정을 나타내는 분사

1 현재분사 (-ing) : 주어가 사물이거나 원인을 제공하는 경우

The movie was very **touching**. 그 영화는 매우 감동적이었어.

2 과거분사 (p.p.) : 주어가 감정을 느끼는 주체인 사람인 경우

The movie was very good, so I was **touched**. 영화가 매우 좋아서 난 감동받았어.

현재분사 (-ing)		과거분사 (p.p.)	
satisfying	만족을 주는	satisfied	만족하는
frustrating	좌절감을 주는	frustrated	좌절감을 느낀, 좌절한
embarrassing	난처하게 하는	embarrassed	당황스러운, 난처한
annoying	짜증스러운	annoyed	짜증이 난
frightening	무서운	frightened	겁이 난
irritating	화나게 하는	irritated	화가 난
disappointing	실망스러운	disappointed	실망한
depressing	우울하게 하는	depressed	우울한
confusing	혼란스럽게 하는	confused	혼란스러워 하는

Simple Test

다음 중 어법에 맞는 것을 고르시오.

1 떠오르는 태양은 우리의 희망을 상징한다.

→ The (rising / risen) sun represents our hope.

2 그 연극은 특수 효과에도 불구하고 매우 지루했다.

→ The play was very (boring / bored) in spite of the special effects.

3 나는 어제 위층의 층간 소음 때문에 짜증이 났다.

→ I was (annoying / annoyed) because of the upstairs floor noise yesterday.

Practice Test

정답 p.15

What's your score? ○   개 X   개

다음 괄호 안의 주어진 단어를 이용하여 문장을 완성하세요.

1 화가 난 그 소년은 급히 집으로 뛰어갔다. (irritate, rapidly)

_____

2 작은 종이배 하나가 물 위에 떠 있다. (paper ship, float)

_____

3 나는 오늘 오후에 매우 흥미진진한 소설을 한 권 샀다. (excite, novel)

_____

4 그들은 그 건물 옥상에서 나무들에 물을 주고 있었다. (on the rooftop, water)

_____

5 나의 아버지는 길거리에 버려진 개를 집으로 데리고 오셨다. (abandon, bring)

_____

6 Jeremy의 보고서는 간략했지만 매우 만족스러웠다. (report, brief, it, satisfy, but)

_____

7 굴욕감을 주는 처벌은 학생들에게 바람직하지 않다. (humiliating, punishment, desirable)

_____

8 나무를 오르려고 뛰고 있는 다람쥐를 봐. (climb the tree, jump, trying, squirrel)

_____

9 땅에 어질러진 깡통들을 재활용 통에 넣자. (put, litter, recycling bin)

_____

10 잠자는 사자의 코털을 건드리지 마라. (잠자는 개를 혼자 둬라.) (let, dogs, alone)

_____

Actual Test

What's your score? O   개 X   개

다음 괄호 안의 주어진 단어를 이용하여 문장을 완성하세요.

1 모든 살아있는 생물을 사랑하는 게 어때? (why don't, live, creatures)

_____

2 그 모든 후보자들은 사람들이 만족하기를 원했다. (candidate, satisfy)

_____

3 나는 어렸을 적에 캐릭터들을 그리는 것에 흥미가 있었다. (interest, in, draw, characters)

_____

4 그 상황이 혼란스러워서 우리는 매우 혼란스러웠다. (situation, confuse)

_____

5 어젯밤에 그 두 소년은 어두운 숲속에서 겁을 먹었다. (the strange, frighten)

_____

6 많은 놀라운 일들이 지난여름에 나에게 일어났다. (many, happen, things)

_____

7 보물찾기(The Treasure Hunt)는 많은 아이들을 흥분시켰고, 그들은 기뻐했다. (excite, many, please)

_____

8 Sally의 반에는 5명의 매우 성가신 소년들이 있다. (there, annoy, class)

_____

9 David는 좌절한 학생들을 진심으로 격려했다. (frustrate, encourage, sincerely)

_____

10 오늘 내가 응원하는 야구팀이 경기에서 졌기 때문에 난 매우 우울하다. (depress, because, that I support)

_____

New Words

rise 뜨다 | represent 나타내다, 상징하다 | in spite of ~에도 불구하고 | floor noise 층간 소음 | rooftop 옥상 | abandon 버리다, 유기하다 | brief 간략한 | humiliate 굴욕감을 주다 | punishment 처벌 | desirable 바람직한 | litter 어지르다, 어지럽히다 | recycling bin 재활용 통 | float 떠오르다 | support 응원하다 | candidate 후보자 | encourage 격려하다 | sincerely 진심으로

14 분사구문

Ⓐ 분사구문이란 무엇인가?

「접속사 + 주어 + 동사」를 동사-ing로 단순하게 전환시키는 구문이다. 이때, 분사구문은 부사의 역할을 한다.

Ⓑ 분사구문의 종류

시간	~할 때	**Cooking some food**, you'd better be careful with the gas stove. = **When** you cook some food, you'd better be careful with the gas stove. 　네가 요리를 할 때 가스레인지를 조심하는 게 좋을 거야.
이유	~이기 때문에	**Being very tall**, he can join the basketball team. = **Since** he is very tall, he can join the basketball team. 　그는 키가 매우 크기 때문에 그 농구팀에 들어갈 수 있다.
조건	만약 ~라면	**Turning left**, you will find the building that you asked about. = **If** you turn left, you will find the building that you asked about. 　왼쪽으로 돌면 너는 네가 물어본 그 건물을 발견할 것이다.
동시동작 ·연속동작	~하면서 / ~하고 나서	**Smiling for joy**, she called her mom.　기쁨으로 미소 지으면서 그녀는 엄마에게 전화를 걸었다. = **As** she smiled for joy, she called her mom. **Taking a walk**, he bought a cup of coffee.　산책을 하고 나서 그는 커피 한 잔을 샀다. = He took a walk, **and** he bought a cup of coffee.
양보	비록 ~일지라도	**Having studied hard**, he failed the test.　그는 열심히 공부했음에도 불구하고 시험에 떨어졌다. = **Although** he had studied hard, he failed the test.
결과	그래서, 그 결과	She spoke too loudly, **surprising everyone**. = She spoke too loudly, **so** she surprised everyone. 　그녀는 너무 크게 말해서 (그 결과) 모든 사람을 놀라게 했다.

Ⓒ 주의해야 할 분사구문

1 완료형 분사구문 : 주절보다 한 시제 앞선 경우 「Having + p.p.」를 쓴다.

Having had a lot of coffee, she didn't need to have any more.

= **As** she had had a lot of coffee, she didn't need to have any more.

　커피를 많이 마셨기 때문에 그녀는 더 마실 필요가 없었다.

2 주절과 부사절의 주어가 다를 경우 : 의미상 주어를 분사 앞에 쓰면 된다.

Terry being sick, his mom took care of him all day long.

= **As** Terry was sick, his mom took care of him all day long.　Terry가 아팠기 때문에 그의 엄마가 하루 종일 그를 돌봤다.

Not knowing her address …

📌 분사구문의 부정형은 Not [Never] + 동사원형-ing이다.

　ex　Not knowing her address, he couldn't send the package. 그녀의 주소를 몰랐기 때문에 그는 그 소포를 보낼 수 없었다.

Ⓓ with 분사구문

1 with + 목적어 + -ing (현재분사) : 능동의 의미 '~한 채로'

She jogged **with her puppy following her**.　그녀는 강아지가 그녀를 따라오게 한 채로 조깅을 했다.

2 with + 목적어 + p.p.(과거분사) : 수동의 의미 '~된 채로'

He studied **with the window closed**.　그는 창문이 닫힌 채로 공부를 했다.

Practice Test

분사구문을 사용해서 다음 우리말을 영작하세요.

1 Michael은 음악을 들으면서 버스를 기다리고 있었다. (wait for)

_____

2 지훈(Jihun)은 그의 새 휴대전화를 쥐고 잠이 들었다. (hold, fall asleep)

_____

3 첫 월급을 타면, 나는 새 노트북을 살 것이다. (get, my first paycheck, laptop)

_____

4 누군가에게 전화를 걸면서 그 은행원은 그 돈을 세었다. (bank teller, someone, count)

_____

5 그는 너무 어리기 때문에 혼자서 버스를 탈 수 없다. (take, by himself)

_____

6 그 사자들은 배가 고프지 않았기 때문에 그저 낮잠을 잤다. (just, take a nap)

_____

7 그는 피자 한 조각을 마저 먹고 나서 이를 닦았다. (finish, brush his teeth)

_____

8 학교에 늦지 않았기 때문에 그는 아침 식사를 할 충분한 시간이 있었다. (not, have)

_____

9 많은 군인들을 잃었기 때문에 그들은 더 이상 싸울 수 없었다. (soldier, anymore)

_____

10 그가 매우 무례했기 때문에 그 선생님은 그의 어머니께 즉시 전화를 했다. (rude, immediately)

_____

Actual Test

What's your score? ○   개   X   개

분사구문을 사용해서 다음 우리말을 영작하세요.

1 그 학회에 참석한다면 너는 많은 정보를 얻을 것이다. (attend, conference)

_____

2 그 기차가 출발했기 때문에 그들은 다음 기차를 기다려야 했다. (depart, wait for)

_____

3 그녀는 Teddy가 길 위에서 그녀를 기다리게 한 채로 집으로 갔다. (with, wait for)

_____

4 그 소년은 그의 가방을 자신의 어깨에 걸친 채로 그 버스를 탔다. (with, backpack, get on, sling, over)

_____

5 그가 그 꽃들에 물을 정기적으로 주었기 때문에 그것들은 지금 꽃을 피우고 있다. (water, regularly, bloom)

_____

6 네가 해변에서 새 가게를 연다면 많은 친구들이 그곳을 방문할 것이다. (open, at the beach)

_____

7 운동을 전혀 하지 않았기 때문에 Steve는 쉽게 피곤함을 느꼈고 에너지가 부족했다. (exercise, at all, lack)

_____

8 그들이 새로운 해결책을 찾지 못했기 때문에 그는 오후에 회의를 소집했다. (solution, call a meeting)

_____

9 그들은 충분한 돈이 없었기 때문에 그들의 아들을 독일로 보낼 수 없었다. (enough, send, Germany)

_____

10 상사가 그에게 또 다른 기회를 주지 않았기 때문에 그의 팀원들이 그 상사에게 말하러 갔다.
(boss, another chance, team members, talk)

_____

New Words

fall asleep 잠이 들다 | paycheck 급료, 월급 | bank teller 은행원 | count (수를) 세다 | take a nap 낮잠을 자다 | immediately 즉시 | not ~ at all 전혀 ~하지 않다 | lack 부족하다 | depart 출발하다 | wait for ~을 기다리다 | slung sling(걸다, 매다)의 과거형 | give up 포기하다 | solution 해결책 | call a meeting 회의를 소집하다

Correcting Errors Ⅰ

What's your score? O   개 X   개

다음 우리말과 같은 뜻이 되도록 어색한 부분을 바르게 고쳐 문장을 다시 쓰시오.

1   Can you repair the breaking machine as soon as possible?

→ _____

너는 그 고장난 기계를 가능한 한 빨리 고칠 수 있니?

2   The story that you sent yesterday was very touched.

→ _____

네가 어제 보내준 그 이야기는 매우 감동적이었어.

3   The food at the new restaurant is disappointed.

→ _____

그 새로운 식당의 음식은 실망스럽다.

4   The passengers were annoying because of the flight delay.

→ _____

그 승객들은 그 비행기 지연으로 인해 짜증이 났다.

5   While fly the kite to the sky, the boy called his friends.

→ _____

하늘로 연을 날리면서 그 소년은 그의 친구들을 불렀다.

6   Being turned right, you can find a public library.

→ _____

오른쪽으로 돌면 너는 공공 도서관을 찾을 수 있다.

7   Having studying too much, she took a rest for a while.

→ _____

공부를 너무 많이 했었기 때문에 그녀는 잠시 동안 휴식을 취했다.

8   Understanding not their language, he looked up the dictionary.

→ _____

그들의 언어를 이해하지 못했기 때문에 그는 사전을 찾아보았다.

Corrrecting Errors ❷

다음 글에서 어색한 부분을 올바르게 고쳐 전체 글을 다시 쓰시오.

The Reason for Different Price

1 There are two stores selling this wine. The price been different between two stores, many people wonder about the wine's quality. Sold the same product, they should have set the same price.

2 But store A's wine is much cheaper than store B's. Reduced the costs of distribution, store A can sell cheaper wine.

3 The quality is the same. The problem is the process. Reducing not the costs of distribution, store B has to sell the wine to consumers at a more expensive price than store B.

4 Which store do you want to buy from?

The Reason for Different Price

1

2

3

4

New Words

sell 팔다, 판매하다 │ wine 포도주, 와인 │ between ~ 사이 [중간]에 │ wonder 궁금하다 │ quality 품질 │ product 상품 │ set the price 값을 정하다 │ much (비교급, 최상급 수식) 훨씬 │ reduce 줄이다, 축소하다 │ process 과정 │ the costs of distribution 유통 비용 │ consumer 소비자 │ cheap 싼 │ expensive 비싼

Paragraph Writing

필요한 부분에 현재분사, 과거분사, 분사구문을 적절히 사용하여 다음 글을 영작하세요.

말썽꾸러기 천재들

1 토머스 에디슨(Thomas Edison)은 호기심이 많았기 때문에 그는 어릴 적에 많은 특별한 행동들을 했다. 그가 병아리들이 부화하는 것을 보기 위해서 달걀을 품은 것은 유명한 일화 중 하나이다.

2 그는 실험 결과가 실망스러웠을 때에도 더 많은 실험들을 계획했다. 많은 사람들을 성가시게 했기 때문에 그는 말썽꾸러기로 불렸다.

3 포드 자동차 회사(Ford Motor Company)의 창시자인 헨리 포드(Henry Ford) 역시 어렸을 때 말썽꾸러기였다. 그는 에디슨보다 16년 늦게 태어났다.

Thomas Edison   Henry Ford

4 어느 날, 그는 에디슨의 저녁 만찬에 초대받았고, 에디슨에게 몇 가지 질문을 했다. 에디슨이 그에게 좋은 충고를 해 주었기 때문에 헨리 포드는 포드 자동차 회사를 설립할 수 있었다. 에디슨의 격려로 헨리 포드는 계속해서 차를 만들었다.

Genius Troublemakers

Help!

genius 천재 | troublemaker 말썽꾸러기 | curiosity 호기심 | do special things 특별한 행동을 하다 | chick 병아리 | hatch 부화하다 | sit on eggs 알을 품다 | episode 일화 | one of ~중 하나 | the result of an experiment 실험결과 | bother 괴롭히다 | founder 창시자 | advice 조언, 충고

Chapter

8

가정법

UNIT 15 가정법 과거와 가정법 과거완료

A 가정법 과거

1 쓰임 : 현재 사실의 반대나 현재에 이루어질 수 없는 일을 나타낼 때

2 해석 : '만약 ~라면[한다면] ~할 텐데'

3 형태 : 「If + S + 동사의 과거형 ~, S + 조동사의 과거형 + 동사원형」

If I **had** 25 hours a day, I **would make** another plan.
만약 내가 하루에 25시간이 있다면 나는 다른 계획을 세울 텐데.

If he **were** taller than you, he **could join** the volleyball club instead of you.
만약 그가 너보다 키가 크다면 너 대신에 배구클럽에 들어갈 수 있을 텐데.

📌 be동사는 were를 쓴다.

If I were …

부러워…   좋겠어…
부럽다…   좋겠다…

B 가정법 과거완료

1 쓰임 : 과거 사실의 반대나 과거에 불가능했던 일을 나타낼 때

2 해석 : '만약 ~였다면[했더라면] ~했을 텐데'

3 형태 : 「If + S + had p.p. ~, S + 조동사의 과거형 + have p.p.」

If he **had had** enough time, he **would have finished** it.
그가 충분한 시간이 있었다면 그것을 끝낼 수 있었을 텐데.

If I **had been born** in the U.S., I **could have spoken** English on my trip.
내가 미국에서 태어났더라면 여행에서 영어를 말할 수 있었을 텐데.

Simple Test

다음 중 어법에 맞는 것을 고르시오.

1 내가 빨리 달릴 수 있다면 축구선수가 될 텐데.
→ If I (run / ran) fast, I would be a soccer player.

2 만약 그녀가 일본에 있다면 내가 그녀를 방문할 텐데.
→ If she (were / has been) in Japan, I would visit her.

3 내가 아프지 않았더라면 그들과 함께 즐거운 시간을 가졌을 텐데.
→ If I (was not / had not been) sick, I would have had fun with them.

4 그 사고가 일어나지 않았더라면 그는 다치지 않았을 텐데.
→ If the accident had not occurred, he would not (have been / be) hurt.

5 그들이 그 규칙을 지켰다면 그때 그들은 후회하지 않았을 텐데.
→ If they had followed the rules, they would not (have / have had) regrets then.

Practice Test

What's your score? O 　 개 X 　 개

가정법 과거, 가정법 과거완료를 사용해서 다음 우리말을 영작하세요.

1　내가 너라면 당장 그 차를 팔 텐데. (sell, right now)

_____

2　그가 이기적이지 않다면 많은 사람들이 그를 좋아할 텐데. (selfish, many)

_____

3　내가 유명한 가수라면 많은 콘서트를 가질 텐데. (famous)

_____

4　그 현명한 여자가 나의 여자 친구라면 나는 행복할 텐데. (wise, woman)

_____

5　그가 커피를 많이 마시지 않았다면 일찍 자러 갈 수 있었을 텐데. (a lot of, go to bed)

_____

6　그 사슴이 배가 고프지 않았다면 그 덫에 걸리지 않았을 텐데. (be caught in the trap)

_____

7　그가 많은 돈을 가지고 있지 않았다면 그들은 그를 속이지 않았을 텐데. (had, deceive)

_____

8　Tony가 그때 독서를 좋아했다면 그 책을 이미 다 읽었을 텐데. (reading books, already)

_____

9　내 차가 있었다면 나는 그녀를 그 파티에 데려다 줄 수 있었을 텐데. (had, my own, take, to)

_____

10　그녀가 컴퓨터에 대해 잘 안다면 그녀의 고장 난 컴퓨터를 고칠 수 있을 텐데. (about, broken, fix)

_____

Actual Test

What's your score? O 개 X 개

가정법 과거, 가정법 과거완료를 사용해서 다음 우리말을 영작하세요.

1 지금 비가 내린다면 미세먼지가 사라질 텐데. (fine dust, raining, disappear)

_____

2 그들이 이 위기를 해결한다면 그들은 훨씬 더 강해질 텐데. (solve, crisis, much)

_____

3 그가 그 약을 먹었다면 더 빨리 회복할 수 있었을 텐데. (had the medicine, recover, faster)

_____

4 그들이 안전벨트를 착용했더라면 그 사고에서 크게 다치지 않았을 텐데.
(fasten their seat belts, be badly hurt, in the accident)

_____

5 만약 축구를 할 수 없다면 그 소년들은 여가 시간에 심심할 텐데. (there, bored, in their free time)

_____

6 그가 그 보고서를 제출하지 않았다면 많은 사람들이 오늘밤에 야근을 했을 텐데.
(report, submit, many, work overtime, tonight)

_____

7 내가 그림을 잘 그린다면 그녀의 초상화를 그릴 수 있을 텐데. (good at, draw, portrait)

_____

8 그녀가 빵을 좋아한다면 그 제빵사가 그녀에게 많은 빵을 줄 텐데. (baker, a lot of)

_____

9 만약 교통 체증이 없었다면, 우리는 목적지에 제때 도착할 수 있었을 텐데.
(there, a traffic jam, reach our destination, on time)

_____

10 우리 동네에 편의점이 없었더라면 우리는 지난밤 늦게 우유를 살 수 없었을 텐데. (any convenience stores, in)

_____

New Words

instead of ~ 대신에 | regret 후회하다; 후회 | be caught in a trap 덫에 걸리다 | deceive 속이다 | selfish 이기적인 | fine dust 미세먼지 | crisis 위기 | recover 회복하다 | fasten one's seat belt 안전벨트를 매다 | work overtime 시간외로 일하다 | destination 목적지 | convenience store 편의점 | neighborhood 동네

UNIT 16 여러 가지 가정법

A I wish 가정법

1 **I wish 가정법 과거 :** 소망하는 시점과 소망하는 내용의 시점이 일치한다.

I wish + 주어 + 동사의 과거형	'~라면 좋을 텐데'
I wished + 주어 + 동사의 과거형	'~라면 좋았을 텐데'

I wish I **had** enough time to visit my family in Korea.
내가 한국에 있는 가족을 방문할 충분한 시간이 있으면 좋을 텐데.

I wished I **could** speak a foreign language fluently. 내가 외국어를 유창하게 말할 수 있다면 좋았을 텐데.

2 **I wish 가정법 과거완료 :** 소망하는 시점보다 소망하는 내용의 시점이 앞선다.

I wish + 주어 + had p.p.	'~했다면 좋을 텐데'
I wished + 주어 + had p.p.	'~했다면 좋았을 텐데'

I wish I **had saved** the important file on my USB. 내가 그 중요한 파일을 나의 USB에 저장했다면 좋을 텐데.

I wished you **had arrived** here before 10 a.m. 네가 오전 10시 전에 여기 도착했다면 좋았을 텐데.

B as if 가정법 (= as though)

1 **as if 가정법 과거 :** '마치 ~인[하는] 것처럼'

· 「주어 + 동사의 현재형/과거형 as if + 주어 + 동사의 과거형」

둘 다 내꺼

He **talks as if** he **had** two expensive cars.
그는 마치 비싼 자동차 두 대를 가지고 있는 것처럼 말한다.

📌 주절과 동일한 시점일 때

2 **as if 가정법 과거완료 :** '마치 ~였던[했던] 것처럼'

· 「주어 + 동사의 현재형/과거형 as if + 주어 + had p.p.」

He **continued** adding the numbers mentally **as if** he **had had** a calculator.
그는 마치 계산기를 가지고 있었던 것처럼 마음속으로 숫자들을 계속 더했다.

📌 주절보다 앞선 시점일 때

C Without, But for + 명사, 가정법 과거 / 과거완료

1 Without = But for = If it were not for = Were it not for : '~이 없다면'

Without TV, his life **would be** boring. TV가 없다면 그의 삶은 지루할 텐데.

= **But for** TV, his life **would be** boring. = **If it were not for** TV, his life **would be** boring.

= **Were it for** TV, his life **would be** boring.

2 Without = But for = If it had not been for = Had it not been for : '~이 없었다면'

Without his help, they **couldn't have survived** the accident.

= **But for** his help, they **couldn't have survived** the accident.

= **If it had not been for** his help, they **couldn't have survived** the accident.

= **Had it not been for** his help, they **couldn't have survived** the accident.

그의 도움이 없었다면 그들은 그 사고에서 살아남을 수 없었을 텐데.

Practice Test

What's your score? O   개   X   개

가정법 구문을 사용해서 다음 우리말을 영작하세요.

1 내가 만화가라면 좋을 텐데. (wish, cartoonist)

_____

2 내가 몰디브(the Maldives)에 있다면 좋을 텐데. (I wish)

_____

3 그녀는 마치 모든 것을 아는 것처럼 말한다. (as if)

_____

4 영화가 없다면 나의 삶은 지루할 텐데. (without, would, boring)

_____

5 내가 나의 할머니께 전화를 더 많이 드렸다면 좋을 텐데. (I wish, more)

_____

6 커피가 없다면 나는 매일 졸릴 텐데. (but for, feel sleepy)

_____

7 Steve는 마치 그가 테니스 선수인 것처럼 말한다. (as if)

_____

8 그는 그가 노래를 잘 하는 것처럼 항상 말한다. (as if, good at)

_____

9 사랑이 없다면 사람들은 행복하지 않을 것이다. (if it were not for)

_____

10 전 세계의 나쁜 사람들이 사라진다면 좋을 텐데. (I wish, people in the world, disappear)

_____

Actual Test

What's your score? O 개 X 개

가정법 구문을 사용해서 다음 우리말을 영작하세요.

1 내가 그 가난한 어린이들과 더 많은 시간을 보냈다면 좋을 텐데. (I wish, spend)

_____

2 그는 마치 그 답을 알았던 것처럼 미소 지었다. (as if, the answer)

_____

3 모든 사람들이 그 결과에 만족했다면 좋았을 텐데. (I wished, satisfied, everybody)

_____

4 그녀는 마치 겁에 질린 것처럼 크게 소리쳤다. (loudly, as though, frightened)

_____

5 그는 좋은 직장에 취직했던 것처럼 행복해 보였다. (as if, get a job, in)

_____

6 그 의사는 세상의 모든 질병들이 존재하지 않기를 소망했다. (wished, diseases, exist)

_____

7 그의 리더십이 없었다면 우리는 그 심각한 상황을 벗어날 수 없었을 텐데. (were it not for, escape, situation)

_____

8 그 소방대원의 도움이 없었다면 Philip은 그 사고에서 살아남지 못했을 것이다. (but for, fireman, survive)

_____

9 그녀는 마치 모든 드라마를 봤던 것처럼 많은 이야기들을 알고 있다. (as though, all the dramas)

_____

10 휴대전화가 없다면 많은 십 대들이 더 많이 이야기를 나눌 수 있을 텐데. (were it not for, communicate)

_____

New Words

calculator 계산기 │ feel sleepy 졸리다 │ cartoonist 만화가 │ escape 벗어나다, 도피하다 │ situation 상황 │ loudly 큰 소리로 │
disappear 사라지다 │ frightened 놀란, 겁에 질린 │ disease 질병 │ exist 존재하다 │ get a job 취직하다

Correcting Errors Ⅰ

What's your score? O   개   X   개

다음 우리말과 같은 뜻이 되도록 어색한 부분을 바르게 고쳐 문장을 다시 쓰시오.

1   If I am you, I would apply for the company.

→ _____

내가 너라면 그 회사에 지원할 텐데.

2   If he had a lot of time, he can prepare the report much better.

→ _____

그가 많은 시간이 있다면 그 보고서를 훨씬 더 잘 준비할 텐데.

3   If they had had a lot of money, they could buy that building.

→ _____

그들이 만약 많은 돈을 가졌었더라면 저 건물을 살 수 있었을 텐데.

4   If the policeman were in the bank, he could have caught the thief.

→ _____

만약 그 경찰이 그 은행 안에 있었더라면 그는 그 도둑을 잡을 수 있었을 텐데.

5   I wish that I can compose beautiful songs.

→ _____

내가 아름다운 노래들을 작곡할 수 있다면 좋을 텐데.

6   I wish I had breakfast before the meeting this morning.

→ _____

오늘 아침 그 회의 전에 아침식사를 했더라면 좋을 텐데.

7   Sarah talks as if she known everything about her.

→ _____

Sarah는 마치 그녀에 대해 모든 것을 알고 있는 것처럼 말한다.

8   It were not for the navigation systems, we couldn't drive conveniently.

→ _____

네비게이션 시스템이 없다면, 우리는 편안하게 운전할 수 없을 텐데.

작성일자 : _____ 월 _____ 일

다음 글에서 잘못된 부분을 올바르게 고쳐 전체 글을 다시 쓰시오.

I wish ...

1 Hi, my name is John. I live in Korea. I have a dream. I really want to speak English well. I wish I was born in Canada.

2 If I am living in Canada, I would speak English very well. My younger brother Sam usually talks as if he speaks English very well. But I know how poor his spoken English is.

3 But with an English dictionary, I could not speak and write English well. I would like to speak English well. So every day I will repeat many times five English expressions. I think that going to Canada is a good way to speak English better.

4 I wish I could lived in beautiful Canada. If you get a chance to go there, please take me with you!

I wish ...

1

2

3

4

New Words

spoken 말로 하는, 구두의 | dictionary 사전 | repeat 반복하다 | many times 여러 번 | expression 표현 | way 방법, 방식 | get a chance 기회를 얻다 | take 데리고 가다

Paragraph Writing

작성일자 : _____월 _____일

필요한 부분에 가정법 구문을 적절히 사용하여 다음 글을 영작하세요.

볼링 동호회

1 나는 볼링을 치러 가는 것을 좋아한다. 나는 이 도시에 있는 볼링 동호회 회원 중 한 명이다. 우리 볼링 동호회에는 많은 사람들이 있다. 여러분에게 몇 명의 친구들을 소개한다.

2 Tom! 그는 그가 더 어렸을 때 마치 전문적인 볼링 선수였던 것처럼 항상 말한다. 나는 그가 몇몇 영상이나 사진을 우리에게 보여준다면 그것을 증명할 수 있다고 생각한다. Kevin! 만약 내가 Kevin이라면 많은 볼링 대회에 참가할 텐데. 그는 볼링을 매우 잘 친다. Ben! 장기간 훈련들이 없다면, 그는 200점 이상 득점을 할 수 없을 것이다. 그는 마치 그가 프로선수인 것처럼 매일 연습한다. Terry! 그는 볼링을 못 친다. 볼링을 칠 때마다 그는 마치 전에 한 번도 볼링을 쳐 본적이 없었던 사람 같다.

3 볼링을 칠 때마다 나는 그것을 그저 즐기기를 원한다. 볼링이 없다면, 나는 행복하지 않을 것이다.

My Bowling Club

Help!

prove 증명하다 | competition 대회 | professional 직업으로 하는, 프로의 | whenever ~할 때마다 | bowl (볼링 경기에서) 공을 굴리다, 볼링을 치다 | bowler 볼링 선수 | score ~의 득점을 하다 | be poor at ~을 못하다

Chapter

9

주요 구문

UNIT 17 · 비교 구문

A 원급을 이용한 표현

1 as 형용사 [부사] as : '~만큼 ~한[하게]' 📌 부정형 : not as[so] 형용사[부사] as

Diligence is **as** important **as** ability. 부지런함은 능력만큼 중요하다.

This library is not **as[so]** new **as** my school library. 이 도서관은 우리 학교 도서관만큼 새롭지 않다.

= My school library is **newer than** this library. 우리 학교 도서관은 이 도서관보다 더 새롭다.

2 as 형용사 [부사] as possible : '가능한 한 ~한[하게]'

The thief ran away **as** fast **as possible**. 그 도둑은 가능한 한 빨리 도망갔다.

= The thief ran away **as** fast **as he could**. 📌 as 형용사[부사] as 주어 can[could]

B 비교급을 이용한 표현

1 the 비교급 ~, the 비교급 ~ : '~하면 할수록 더 ~한'

The more books you read, **the more** knowledge you get. 더 많은 책을 읽을수록 더 많은 지식을 얻는다.

2 비교급 and 비교급 : '점점 더 ~한'

The weather is getting **colder and colder**. 날씨가 점점 더 추워지고 있다.

C 최상급을 이용한 표현

최상급 + in + 단수 / 최상급 + of + 복수

He is **the most** handsome boy **in** my class. 그는 우리 반에서 가장 잘생겼다.

She is **the tallest** girl **of** the three. 그녀는 세 명 중에 가장 키가 크다.

colder and colder

D 상관접속사 구문

both A and B	A와 B 둘 다	항상 복수 취급
either A or B	A와 B 둘 중 하나	B에 수 일치
neither A nor B	A와 B 둘 다 아닌	B에 수 일치
not A but B	A가 아니라 B	B에 수 일치
not only A but (also) B = B as well as A	A뿐만 아니라 B도	B에 수 일치

Simple Test

다음 중 어법에 맞는 것을 고르시오.

1 이 책은 그 게임만큼이나 흥미롭다.

→ This book is as (interesting / more interesting) as the game.

2 그들은 가능한 한 많은 지원자를 만나기 원한다.

→ They want to meet as many applicants as (possible / they do).

3 더 많이 운동할수록 더 건강해질 수 있다.

→ The more you exercise, (healthier / the healthier) you can be.

4 그와 나 둘 다 그 형편없는 결과에 책임이 없다.

→ Neither he nor I (am / are) responsible for the poor result.

Practice Test

What's your score? O   개 X   개

비교 구문을 사용해서 다음 우리말을 영작하세요.

1   그 공원은 내가 예상했던 것만큼 크지 않다. (as, expect)

_____

2   그들은 가능한 한 빨리 그 조사를 끝냈다. (possible, investigation, quickly)

_____

3   그는 의사가 아니라 간호사이다. (not, but)

_____

4   모든 것이 점점 더 좋아졌다. (everything, get, and)

_____

5   너와 Carl 둘 중 하나가 거기에 가야 한다. (either, have to)

_____

6   건강 검진 때문에 너희들뿐만 아니라 나도 물을 전혀 마실 수 없다.
(not only, any, because of, the health check-ups)

_____

7   그들은 에어컨뿐만 아니라 선풍기도 사용했다. (air conditioner, fan, as well)

_____

8   이 건물은 이 모든 건물 중에서 가장 오래되었다. (all, these, oldest)

_____

9   경찰관과 소방관 모두 그들을 안전하게 구조했다. (police officers, firefighters, both, rescue)

_____

10   날씨가 시원해질수록 더 많은 사람들이 종종 소풍을 간다. (it, cool, go on picnics)

_____

Actual Test ⭐⭐

비교 구문을 사용해서 다음 우리말을 영작하세요.

1 더 많이 이해할수록 세상은 더 좋아질 것이다. (understand, will)

_____

2 우리는 긍정적일수록 더 행복해진다. (become, positive)

_____

3 요즈음에 환경오염이 점점 더 심각해지고 있다. (environmental pollution, get, serious)

_____

4 내가 아니라 그녀가 해저 탐사에 관심이 있다. (underwater exploration, interested in)

_____

5 그 보아뱀은 그 정글에서 가장 위협적인 동물이다. (boa constrictor, threatening)

_____

6 James는 그 학생들 중에 가장 도전적이고 성실한 소년이다. (challenging, faithful)

_____

7 그 위원회는 진보적이지도 않고 보수적이지도 않다. (committee, conservative, progressive)

_____

8 그 외과의사는 바둑기사만큼이나 신중하다. (surgeon, as, Baduk player, careful)

_____

9 그들은 가능한 한 조용히 그 개의 장례를 치렀다. (have a funeral for, possible, quietly)

_____

10 지구 온난화뿐만 아니라 불법 사냥도 전 세계적으로 중요한 문제이다.
(global warming, illegal hunting, global issue, as well)

_____

New Words

applicant 지원자 | be responsible for ~에 책임이 있다 | investigation 조사 | go on a picnic 소풍 가다 |
air conditioner 에어컨 | fan 선풍기 | environmental pollution 환경오염 | exploration 탐사, 탐험 | global warming
지구 온난화 | illegal hunting 불법 사냥 | boa constrictor 보아뱀 | threatening 위협적인 | challenging 도전적인 |
faithful 성실한 | committee 위원회 | progressive 진보적인 | conservative 보수적인 | surgeon 외과의사 | funeral 장례식

UNIT 18 강조, 도치, 동격 구문

A 강조 구문

1 It ~ that... 강조 구문 : 동사를 제외한 주어, 목적어, 부사(구) 등을 강조한다.

📌 that은 강조하는 내용에 따라 who(m), which, when, where 등으로 바꿔 쓸 수 있다.

Sam met Amy at the amusement park by accident last Saturday.
Sam은 지난 토요일에 우연히 놀이공원에서 Amy를 만났다.

→ **It** was **Sam that [who]** met Amy at the amusement park by accident last Saturday.
　지난 토요일에 우연히 놀이공원에서 Amy를 만난 사람은 Sam이었다. (주어 Sam 강조)

→ **It** was **Amy that [who]** Sam met at the amusement park by accident last Saturday.
　Sam이 지난 토요일에 우연히 놀이공원에서 만난 사람은 Amy였다. (목적어 Amy 강조)

→ **It** was **last Saturday that [when]** Sam met Amy at the amusement park by accident.
　Sam이 우연히 놀이공원에서 Amy를 만났던 때는 지난 토요일이었다. (부사구 last Saturday 강조)

2 동사를 강조하는 do [does, did] + 동사원형

He invited the actor to his house. 그는 집에 그 배우를 초대했다.

→ He **did** invite the actor to his house. 그는 집에 정말 그 배우를 초대했다.

3 재귀대명사 강조 : '스스로, 직접'으로 해석하며 생략 가능하다.

He **himself** drew the beautiful landscape. 그는 직접 그 아름다운 풍경화를 그렸다.

📌 so that [in order that] + 주어 + 동사 : '~하도록, ~하기 위해'로 해석하며 목적을 강조할 수 있다.
　ex He left Seoul so that he could build a new house in the countryside.
　　　그는 시골에 새 집을 짓기 위해 서울을 떠났다.

B 도치 구문

1 부정어구 도치 : Never [No, Seldom, Not, Rarely, Little, Only] + (조)동사+주어 ~.

Never **did he** dream of such a fantastic result. 그는 그런 환상적인 결과를 결코 꿈도 꾸지 못했다.

Seldom **does my uncle** drink coffee. 나의 삼촌은 거의 커피를 마시지 않는다.

2 장소 부사구 도치

Julia stood in front of the post office. Julia는 우체국 앞에 서 있었다.

→ In front of the post office **stood Julia**.

The bus stop is next to this building. 그 버스 정류장은 이 건물 옆에 있다.

→ Next to this building **is the bus stop**.

📌 장소 부사구 도치에서 주어가 대명사인 경우는 도치하지 않는다.
　ex In a small city he lives. (O) / In a small city lives he. (X)

C 동격의 that

1 쓰임 : 명사, 대명사를 한번 더 설명하거나 보충하기 위해 사용한다.

2 동격을 나타내는 주요 명사 : fact, news, idea, belief, thought 등

The idea **that** kindness is better than a good first impression is known to me.
좋은 첫인상보다 더 좋은 것이 친절함이라고 나는 알고 있다.

Practice Test

정답 p.21

What's your score? O 개 X 개

강조, 도치, 동격 구문을 사용해서 다음 우리말을 영작하세요.

1 그 토끼는 그 나무 아래에서 낮잠을 잤다. (take a nap)

_____

2 나의 조카는 거의 채소를 먹지 않는다. (nephew, vegetables)

_____

3 그 왕은 친히 그 편지를 그에게 주었다. (himself, to him)

_____

4 아름다운 새가 나뭇가지 위에서 지저귀고 있었다. (twitter, the)

_____

5 그들이 인상적인 공연을 했던 때가 바로 지난 주였다. (that, give, impressive)

_____

6 그가 어제 그녀를 만난 곳은 일본 대사관 앞이었다. (it, Japanese Embassy)

_____

7 그는 그 시험에 합격하는 것을 전혀 예상하지 못했다. (expect, never, to pass)

_____

8 그가 그의 아내와 헤어졌다는 사실은 충격적이다. (separate from, that, shocking)

_____

9 그들은 더 많은 사람들과 소통하기 위해 블로그를 시작했다. (a blog, so that, start, communicate with)

_____

10 그는 정말로 그의 전 재산을 가난한 사람들과 함께 나눴다. (did, share, whole fortune)

_____

Actual Test

정답 p.21

What's your score? O   개 X   개

강조, 도치, 동격 구문을 사용해서 다음 우리말을 영작하세요.

1 그가 채용될 것이라는 믿음은 실현되었다. (would, hire, come true)

_____

2 평가 그 자체는 변경될 수 없다. (assessments, changed)

_____

3 그들이 시장으로 추천한 사람은 바로 Jacob이었다. (it, mayor, recommend, for)

_____

4 그 도서관을 이전하기 위하여 그들은 책들을 분류했다. (could, relocated, in order that, classify)

_____

5 매일 아침 그는 건강을 유지하기 위해 테니스를 친다. (keep fit)

_____

6 그녀는 내일의 과제에 대해 거의 생각하지 않았다. (tomorrow's assignment, little)

_____

7 그 선생님이 학생들에게 무관심하다는 생각은 틀렸다. (indifferent, wrong)

_____

8 그는 많은 돈을 정말로 새 신발을 사는 데 소비했다. (did, on buying)

_____

9 그가 오늘 아침에 그의 지갑을 잃어버린 곳은 바로 버스 정류장이었다. (it, wallet, at the bus stop)

_____

10 그녀는 수집을 위한 옛 가구를 사기 위해 많은 가게들을 방문했다. (collection, so that, furniture, stores)

_____

New Words

by accident 우연히 | landscape 풍경화 | first impression 첫인상 | embassy 대사관 | impressive 인상적인 | separate from ~와 헤어지다 | communicate with ~와 소통하다 | branch 나뭇가지 | twitter 지저귀다 | whole fortune 전 재산 | nephew 조카 | come true 실현되다 | assessment 평가 | recommend 추천하다 | relocate 이전하다 [시키다] | classify 분류하다 | assignment 과제 | furniture 가구 | collection 수집

Correcting Errors Ⅰ

What's your score? O   개   X   개

다음 우리말과 같은 뜻이 되도록 어색한 부분을 바르게 고쳐 문장을 다시 쓰시오.

1 The new smartphone is as innovative than the laptop.

→ _____

그 새로운 스마트폰은 그 노트북만큼 혁신적이다.

2 The scientists wanted to invent the machine as soon as possibly.

→ _____

그 과학자들은 그 기계를 가능한 한 빨리 발명하기를 원했다.

3 The more water we drink, the more healthy we will get.

→ _____

우리가 더 많은 물을 마시면 마실수록, 우리는 더 건강해질 것이다.

4 The boy as well as I have to arrive there on time.

→ _____

나뿐만 아니라 그 소년도 제시간에 거기 도착해야 한다.

5 It was at the bus stop what I first met her last year.

→ _____

내가 작년에 그녀를 처음 만난 곳은 버스 정류장이었다.

6 He does likes to go fishing on weekends.

→ _____

그는 주말마다 낚시하러 가는 것을 정말 좋아한다.

7 Never my dad gave me money for buying concert tickets.

→ _____

아버지는 콘서트 티켓을 사기 위한 돈을 절대 나에게 주지 않으신다.

8 At that time, several people didn't accept the fact which the Earth is round.

→ _____

그때 몇몇 사람들은 지구가 둥글다는 사실을 받아들이지 못했다.

Correcting Errors ⅠⅠ

다음 글에서 잘못된 부분을 올바르게 고쳐 전체 글을 다시 쓰시오.

The Huge Animal

1 In the jungle were there many animals. In the trees some sleeping monkeys were. In the pond some scary alligators were.

2 One day, a huge animal appeared. Its size was as bigger as an elephant. Never had seen the animals in the jungle such a big animal. Monkeys as well as alligators was scared.

3 It was the biggest animal in the jungle. More and many animals gathered to see the huge animal. One of them shouted. "It's not moving. It is not only not moving so not breathing!"

4 One of the brave monkeys shouted again. "It's not an animal but also a huge tent that men have set up for studying our jungle."

The Huge Animal

1

2

3

4

New Words

pond 연못 | scary 무서운, 겁나는 | alligator 악어 | huge 거대한 | appear 나타나다 | as well as ~뿐만 아니라 | gather 모이다 | shout 소리치다 | not A but B A가 아니라 B | breathing 호흡 | set up 세우다, 설립하다

Paragraph Writing

강조, 도치구문을 최대한 사용하여 전체 글을 완성하세요.

나의 첫 발표

1 나는 지난주에 발표를 했다. 그것은 내 인생의 첫 번째 발표였다. 도서관에서 나는 많은 책을 읽었다. 더 많은 책을 읽을수록, 나는 더 편안해졌다.

2 내가 그 발표를 위해 약간의 조언을 구했던 사람은 바로 나의 아버지였다. 나의 아버지께서는 회사에서 많은 발표를 하신다.

3 나는 좋은 원고뿐 아니라 좋은 발표 기술도 필요했다. 그래서 나는 좋은 발표를 하기 위해 가능한 한 많은 영상들을 봤고 매일 연습했다. 마침내, 나는 정말로 좋은 발표를 했다. 나의 발표 후, 많은 선생님들과 학생들이 박수를 쳤다. 나는 다음에 더 좋은 발표를 하기 위해 더 연습할 것이다. 그 이유는 지금 나의 꿈이 뛰어난 아나운서가 되는 것으로 바뀌었기 때문이다.

4 나의 첫 발표 전에는 내가 아나운서가 되고 싶을 거라고 전혀 예상하지 못했다. 여러분도 훌륭한 발표를 준비할 수 있고 잘 발표할 수 있다. 그것은 어렵지 않다

My First Presentation

Final Test

Final Test 1

(1~20) 다음 빈칸에 들어갈 알맞은 단어를 적으세요.

1 그들은 그녀가 그 도시에 무사히 도착하도록 도왔다.

They helped her _____ _____ at the city safely.

2 나는 그들이 우리의 적인지 아닌지를 모른다.

I don't know _____ _____ _____ our enemies or not.

3 그녀는 낯선 도시들을 혼자 방문하는 것을 꺼렸다.

She minded _____ _____ cities _____ herself.

4 우리 가족은 내년이면 20년을 이곳에서 살아온 셈이 된다.

My family _____ _____ _____ here for 20 years next year.

5 Joy는 그녀가 태어났던 도시를 기억하지 못한다.

Joy doesn't remember the city _____ she was born.

6 이 깡통들은 버려질 것이다.

These cans _____ _____ _____ away.

7 그녀의 방은 좋은 향기로 가득 차 있었다.

Her room _____ _____ _____ a good smell.

8 그는 정말 수백 개의 단어들을 암기했다. (do)

He _____ _____ hundreds of words.

9 그 아기가 울고 있었던 곳은 바로 병원이었다.

_____ was at the hospital _____ the baby was crying.

10 그는 키가 컸기 때문에 농구를 잘했다.

_____ _____ , he was good at playing basketball.

11 그는 작년 여름에 부산(Busan)에 갔던 것을 기억하지 못했다.

He couldn't ＿＿＿＿＿＿＿ ＿＿＿＿＿＿＿ to Busan last summer.

12 놀이공원에서 아무것도 하지 않는 것은 매우 드물다. (not)

＿＿＿＿＿＿＿ ＿＿＿＿＿＿＿ ＿＿＿＿＿＿＿ in the amusement park is very unusual.

13 그들은 어제부터 카드를 조금 만들고 있는 중이다.

They ＿＿＿＿＿＿＿ ＿＿＿＿＿＿＿ ＿＿＿＿＿＿＿ some cards since yesterday.

14 그가 여기를 떠났을 것이라고는 꿈도 꾸지 못했다.

Never ＿＿＿＿＿＿＿ I ＿＿＿＿＿＿＿ that he had left here.

15 나는 그들이 그녀에게 말해 준 것을 알지 못했다.

I didn't know ＿＿＿＿＿＿＿ ＿＿＿＿＿＿＿ ＿＿＿＿＿＿＿ her.

16 사람들은 바닷가재가 맛있다고들 한다.

It ＿＿＿＿＿＿＿ ＿＿＿＿＿＿＿ ＿＿＿＿＿＿＿ lobsters are delicious.

17 그는 Steve에게 좋은 자전거를 사 주었다.

He bought a good ＿＿＿＿＿＿＿ ＿＿＿＿＿＿＿ ＿＿＿＿＿＿＿ .

18 그는 집에 도착하자마자 차가운 물 한 컵을 마셨다.

＿＿＿＿＿＿＿ ＿＿＿＿＿＿＿ ＿＿＿＿＿＿＿ he got home, he drank a cup of cold water.

19 그의 주소를 몰랐기 때문에 나는 그의 친구 Tom에게 그것을 보냈다.

＿＿＿＿＿＿＿ ＿＿＿＿＿＿＿ his address, I couldn't send it to his friend Tom.

20 그가 아프지 않았더라면 그는 자신의 숙제를 다 했을 텐데.

＿＿＿＿＿＿＿ he ＿＿＿＿＿＿＿ ＿＿＿＿＿＿＿ ＿＿＿＿＿＿＿ sick, he would have finished his homework.

Final Test 2

(1~20) 다음 괄호 안의 주어진 단어를 이용하여 문장을 완성하세요.

1 공원에서 달리고 있는 그 소녀와 강아지는 내 옆집에 산다. (next door to me, puppy)

_____

2 내가 정말 하고 싶은 것은 1년 동안 여행하는 것이다. (what, really, traveling, for)

_____

3 그가 여기 머무는 한 나는 그를 도울 것이다. (as, stay)

_____

4 그들은 성공하기 위해 오늘 10시간 이상 일을 했다. (so that, over)

_____

5 너희들은 오늘 저 아이들을 돌보기로 되어 있다. (supposed, take care of)

_____

6 승진하는 것은 누구에게나 좋은 일이다. (being, promote, for everyone)

_____

7 우리는 많은 사람이 희생되었던 이 장소를 잊어서는 안 된다. (must, the place, sacrificed)

_____

8 나는 아버지가 유명한 영화배우인 그녀와 저녁식사를 했다. (famous, movie star)

_____

9 매일 노인들을 돕는 것을 보니 그는 매우 친절하다. (it, the elderly, every)

_____

10 나가기 전에 창문들을 닫는 것을 잊지 마. (before going out)

_____

정답 p.22

What's your score? O   개 X   개

11 그는 사무실에 들어가서 신문을 읽었다. (enter, and)

_____

12 그 질문은 많은 학생을 혼란스럽게 했다. (make, confuse)

_____

13 그가 은행에 갔을 때 그곳은 이미 닫혀있었다. (already)

_____

14 내가 집에 도착할 때에 나의 아들은 잠들어 있을 것이다. (get home, fallen asleep)

_____

15 그 영화가 매우 흥미진진해서 우리는 만족했다. (excite, very, so, satisfy)

_____

16 Billy는 예의가 바르기 때문에 많은 선생님들이 그를 좋아한다. (being, polite)

_____

17 만약 내가 두 개의 사과를 갖고 있다면 너에게 하나를 줄 텐데. (if, would)

_____

18 그는 마치 그가 물 위를 걸을 수 있는 것처럼 말한다. (talk, as if, on water)

_____

19 나도 그녀도 골프를 잘 치지 못한다. (nor, good at)

_____

20 그가 자전거를 처음 배웠던 곳은 바로 이 공원에서였다. (it, that, how to, ride)

_____

MEMO

서술형·수행평가 만점을 만드는 좋은 영작 습관!

제대로 영작문

5 정답

DARAKWON

제대로 영작문

5 ---------- 심화

DARAKWON

Chapter 1

문장의 형식

 UNIT 01 1형식, 2형식, 3형식

Simple Test
p.10

1 doesn't
2 entered
3 marry
4 looks

Practice Test
p.11

1 The doctor married the nurse.
2 Everyone turned pale upon seeing the result.
3 The biggest tree in Seoul stands on that hill.
4 They didn't (=did not) know its real value.
5 They kept good relationships with their neighbors.
6 The next train will arrive at 2 p.m. (= The next train will arrive at 2 o'clock in the afternoon.)
7 Many (=A lot of = Lots of) people gave up voting today.
8 There will be just one opportunity for us.
9 This old stamp seems very valuable.
10 Their representative attended the conference.

Actual Test
p.12

1 According to this report, we can't (= cannot) find a better way.
2 We will only have a multiple choice test today.
3 This hat looks too small for your head.
4 We are going to arrive in Bangkok in two

hours.
5 The cappuccino at this cafe tastes fantastic.
6 Everyone can be [become] a poet in this beautiful place.
7 Many (= A lot of = Lots of) professors attended the meeting yesterday.
8 They entered the room without getting permission.
9 The meeting lasted for three hours this morning.
10 We discussed the matter very seriously.

UNIT 02 4형식, 5형식

Simple Test
p.13

1 me happiness
2 for
3 of
4 comfortable

Practice Test
p.14

1 The famous golfer gave me a golf ball.
2 They finally gave freedom to him.
3 Good habits make us diligent.
4 The storekeeper chose good fruits for me.
5 Sally gave a good performance in front of all of the judges.
6 May [Can] I ask you a favor?
7 Money sometimes makes people sad.
8 Let me explain what I did yesterday.
9 Let us go home now.
10 I think Korean dramas fantastic.

Actual Test
p.15

1 They gave many (= a lot of = lots of) presents to the orphanage.
2 Eating nuts makes people much healthier.
3 This new machine will make our work easier.
4 Playing badminton makes my parents much more active.

5 Proverbs will give us good lessons.

6 Staying up late makes us tired.

7 The government named the event "The World Market".

8 Many (= A lot of = Lots of) people thought his invention a miracle.

9 He didn't (= did not) explain this confusing situation to me.

10 The couch thought Sam the best player.

Correcting Errors ①

p.16

1 The students **entered** their classroom quickly.

2 He looks very **sad** today because of bad news.

3 She bought a beautiful house **for** her mother.

4 The teacher asked tough questions **of** his pupils.

5 He had his daughter **do** her homework.

6 They saw the girls **dance [dancing]** on the stage.

7 Can you give the report **to** us? (= Can you give us the report?)

8 She **looks** very tired today.

Correcting Errors ②

p.17

Model Answer

The Interview Day

1 Today, I have **an** (추가) important interview. I have wanted to enter **into** (삭제) the "Giggle" company for a long time. I have applied for a job at the company several times. Finally, today I have an interview.

2 I got up early this morning in order not to be late. Yesterday, **My** (→ **my**) father bought nice shoes **to** (→ **for**) me, and I went **to** (추가) a famous beauty shop in my town to make my hair **beautifully** (→ **beautiful**).

3 But today, I found my hair looked **terribly** (→ **terrible**). Without my mom's help, I couldn't have done anything with my hair.

4 Now, I am very relaxed because I finished the interview. It was **an** (추가) interesting interview. I think I can get a good night's sleep tonight.

해석

면접날

1 오늘 나는 중요한 면접이 있다. 나는 오랫동안 **Giggle** 회사에 들어가고 싶어 해왔고, 그 회사에 여러 번 입사 지원을 했다. 마침내, 오늘 면접이 있다.

2 나는 늦지 않기 위해 오늘 아침 일찍 일어났다. 어제 나의 아버지께서 나에게 좋은 신발을 사주셨고, 나는 내 머리 모양을 아름답게 하기 위해 마을에 있는 유명한 미용실에 갔다.

3 그러나 오늘, 나는 내 머리 모양이 끔찍해 보인다는 것을 발견했다. 엄마의 도움이 없었다면 나는 내 머리 모양을 어떻게 할 수 없었을 것이다.

4 이제 나는 면접을 끝냈기 때문에 매우 마음이 편안하다. 그것은 흥미로운 면접이었다. 나는 오늘 밤에 숙면을 할 수 있다고 생각한다.

Paragraph Writing

p.18

Model Answer

Jessica's Volunteer Work

1 On TV, Jessica saw children dying [die] all over the world. They were suffering from hunger. The program changed her thinking.

2 She wanted to help these poor children. First, she donated some money to them and decided to ask experts what more she could do.

3 Later, she learned about a program for people to visit Africa during their vacations. She decided to go there, but she needed a lot of (= lots of) money. So she worked part-time at a restaurant. Three months later, she got enough money to go to Africa.

4 It'll be her vacation soon. This vacation will give her a very special experience, (= This vacation will give a very special experience to her,) and she will grow up because of that experience.

Chapter 2
명사절과 부사절

UNIT 03 명사절

Simple Test
p.20

1 that
2 if
3 Whether
4 that

Practice Test
p.21

1 We hope (that) they come back safely.
2 Whether she is from Japan (or not) is not important. (= It is not important whether she is from Japan (or not).)
3 She doubted if [whether] they are good people (or not).
4 It is surprising that her hobby is collecting coins. (= That her hobby is collecting coins is surprising.)
5 The idea that coffee is good for your health is strange.
6 I believe that we can (= are able to) escape from here.
7 I wonder whether [if] she can climb that high mountain (or not).
8 The news that subway fare has increased is very disappointing. (= It is very disappointing the news that subway fare has increased.)
9 The main issue is that professors don't have enough time to study.
10 The fact that the firm has a lot of (= lots of = many) problems is not unknown anymore.

Actual Test
p.22

1 Whether he is a tennis player or not is a riddle. (= It is a riddle whether he is a tennis player or not.)
2 The thought that he is our enemy is very dangerous.
3 It is very exceptional for James to eat seafood.
4 I am not sure if [whether] I should wash my car (or not) because the forecast calls for rain. (= Because the forecast calls for rain, I am not sure if [whether] I should wash my car (or not).)
5 My main concern is whether the foreigners can speak Korean (or not).
6 The fact that the singer is married is not known.
7 I wonder whether [if] she eats a lot or not.
8 It is universal that people read the news on the internet these days.
9 The theory that humans evolved from monkeys a long time ago sounds plausible.
10 It is natural that children run here and there all the time.

UNIT 04 부사절

Simple Test
p.23

1 though
2 As soon as
3 since

Practice Test
p.24

1 Unless he is busy, I will ask for his help. (= I will ask for his help unless he is busy.)
2 As soon as Snow White ate an apple, she fell deeply asleep. (= Snow White fell deeply asleep as soon as she ate an apple.)
3 Since he was full, he couldn't eat anything more. (= He couldn't eat anything more since he was full.)

4 As she opened the window, she could feel the refreshing wind. (= She could feel the refreshing wind as she opened the window.)

5 Until the fog cleared, the ships couldn't sail. (= The ships couldn't sail until the fog cleared.)

6 When I forgave Billy, he had already left Korea. (= Billy had already left Korea when I forgave him.)

7 When he called me, I was very surprised at his weak voice. (= I was very surprised at his weak voice when he called me.)

8 Though (= Although = Even though) air is valuable, we can breathe it in for free. (= We can breathe in air for free though (= although = even though) it is valuable.)

9 While the fat man was having a meal, he kept sweating. (= The fat man kept sweating while he was having a meal.)

10 While the professor was calling students' names, I sat on my seat quietly. (= I sat on my seat quietly while the professor was calling students' names.)

Actual Test

1 Whenever he goes to Busan, he eats raw fish. (= He eats raw fish whenever he goes to Busan.)

2 As soon as my younger brother got home, he rushed to the bathroom. (= My younger brother rushed to the bathroom as soon as he got home.)

3 After she lost her wallet, she looked around for it. (= She looked around for her wallet after she lost it.)

4 As soon as he heard the rumor, he told it to his friends. (= He told the rumor to his friend as soon as he heard it.)

5 As long as I am alive, I won't sell this firm. (= I won't sell this firm as long as I am alive.)

6 Since Jinsu is good at playing the guitar, many girls like him. (= Many girls like Jinsu since he is good at playing the guitar.)

7 Because there are many (= a lot of = lots of) mosquitoes, we can't sleep in the house. (= We can't sleep in the house because there are many (= a lot of = lots of) mosquitoes.)

8 When the teacher asks me a question, I am always nervous. (= I am always nervous when the teacher asks me a question.)

9 Once you visit the restaurant, you will be satisfied with the taste of the food. (= You will be satisfied with the taste of the food once you visit the restaurant.)

10 Because the children liked playing in the water, they didn't come out of the tub. (= The children didn't come out of the tub because they liked playing in the water.)

Correcting Errors ❶

1 I wonder **if [whether]** she likes me or not.

2 **That** they are not polite is very disappointing. (= It is very disappointing that they are not polite.)

3 We just stayed inside **because [since, as]** the weather was very bad.

4 **Though [Although, Even though]** I was full, I had more dessert.

5 He exercises every morning in order **that** he loses weight. (= He exercises every morning in order to lose weight.)

6 **Unless he saved** the money, he couldn't buy anything.

7 It is very clear **that** he can't go abroad by himself.

8 The idea **that** people can't live without water is not strange.

Correcting Errors ❷

The Special Prize

1 It is fantastic that my older sister won first prize in the writing contest.

2 As **long** (→ **soon**) as she got home, she

told us about winning first prize. We congratulated her on winning it. **If** (→ **Whether**) she is the best or not is not important for me.

3 My concern is **what** (→ **that**) the prize is very special. It is a brand-new smartphone! But she bought the latest model a few days ago.

4 I have used my cell phone for over three years. I want to change my cell phone. But I am not sure **if or not** (→ **whether or not**) my father and older sister will agree with my idea.

해석

특별한 상

1 나의 누나(언니)가 영작 대회에서 우승한 것은 환상적이다.

2 그녀가 집에 도착하자마자, 그녀는 우승한 것에 대해 우리에게 말했다. 우리는 그녀가 우승한 것을 축하했다. 그녀가 최고인지 아닌지는 나에게는 중요하지 않다.

3 나의 관심은 그 상이 매우 특별하다는 것이다. 그것은 최신형 스마트폰이다. 그러나 그녀는 며칠 전에 최신 모델을 샀다.

4 나는 내 휴대전화를 3년 넘게 사용해왔다. 나는 내 휴대전화를 바꾸기를 원한다. 그러나 나의 아버지와 누나(언니)가 내 의견에 동의할지 아닐지는 확실하지 않다.

Paragraph Writing
p.28

Model Answer

Korean Dramas

1 The fact that Korean dramas are interesting is already well known. Because there are many (= a lot of = lots of) TV broadcasting stations making dramas, people can choose from a lot of good dramas.

2 Once we start watching a drama, we watch it until the last episode. After the first episode, viewers can know whether [if] the drama will succeed (or not). If the first episode gets high ratings, more people are interested in the drama.

3 Before the first episode, many actors make a ratings pledge. If the ratings reach a certain level, they promise to do something to repay their fans. Some actors walk on the street wearing a ridiculous costume, and some have signing events.

4 As long as there are good dramas in Korea, more actors can continue to develop their skills.

Chapter 3

관계사

UNIT 05 관계대명사

Simple Test
p.30

1 who
2 What

Practice Test
p.31

1 I saw a cat which was very aggressive.
2 I met my uncle who is very tall two weeks ago.
3 The child whose eyes were big was smiling at me.
4 What you did last night was really terrific.
5 This is the first prize (that) I have won in the contest.
6 He made a mistake which was irrevocable.
7 Is the lady who is standing in front of that bank your aunt?
8 He invented a strange chair which [that] has only one leg.
9 I invited Amy whose house is really pretty to my birthday party.

10 She showed up at the party wearing a dress whose color was pink.

Actual Test

1 What I really want to do now is drinking a cold Coke. (= Drinking a cold Coke is what I really want to do now.)

2 This is the application which my uncle developed.

3 The boy who [that] was staring at his smartphone stepped in a small puddle.

4 The people who [that] chase only money may fail because of money.

5 This spaghetti whose smell is very good was cooked by my mom.

6 What you did last week was very disappointing. (= It was very disappointing what you did last week.)

7 This is the only project that I got an A grade on from the professor.

8 All these inventions were invented by Steve whose IQ is 154. (= All of these inventions were invented by Steve whose IQ is 154.)

9 I saw several spies, who disappeared in an instant.

10 There were many (= a lot of = lots of) girls and cats that took part in the campaign at Art Park.

 **UNIT 06** 관계부사

Simple Test

1 the way
2 the day that
3 for which
4 the place

Practice Test

1 This is the bank where my father works.
2 Today is (the day) when my parents got married twenty years ago.

3 Tell me the reason (why) Tony doesn't drink milk.

4 This is the way I live.

5 He remembered the stage where he sang a duet with her.

6 Valentine's Day is the day when [that, on which] women give men chocolate. (= Valentine's Day is the day which [that] women give men chocolate on.)

7 The place (where) we go to have a summer vacation should be peaceful.

8 There is no reason why you should go there next week.

9 We will have a wedding the day when [that, on which] I was born. (= We will have a wedding the day which [that] I was born on.)

10 The teacher explained to us how this project was successful.

Actual Test

1 It was the last time when I saw the puppy.

2 Here is the famous restaurant where many (= a lot of = lots of) gourmets eat.

3 She remembered the day when she met her mentor.

4 Here is the town where my grandfather was born.

5 Having a late-night meal is the reason (why) he can't lose any weight. (= Having a late-night meal is (the reason) why he can't lose any weight.)

6 He doesn't (= does not) share the way he bakes delicious bread with other people.

7 Smartphones are the way people can interact with friends abroad easily.

8 The reason (why) many (= a lot of = lots of) people can't succeed is that they are afraid of change.

9 The novice driver couldn't remember how he turned on the blinkers at that time.

10 August 15th is the day when Korea became independent.

Correcting Errors ❶   p.36

1 I remember the boy **whose** mother is a famous writer.

2 Please tell us **what** you saw last night.

3 Is there anything **that** interests you lately?

4 The man has many cars, **which** are very expensive.

5 She knows **the way** she can pass the exam. (= She knows **how** she can pass the exam.)

6 Can you remember the restaurant **where [at(in) which]** we had a great dinner together?

7 Let's go to the zoo **where [at(in) which]** we had a wonderful time.

8 **What** I want to have now is comfortable shoes to run a marathon.

Correcting Errors ❷   p.37

My Childhood Friend

1 I visited somewhere quiet and beautiful last Saturday. The place I visited was my hometown. The reason **how (→ why)** I visited there is to remember my childhood.

2 I met an old man **who (→ whose)** son's name is Jiseok. He was one of my friends when I was young.

3 I remember many times **which (→ when)** I played with Jiseok. We lost contact after I move to Seoul. I asked the old man **the way** how 또는 the way **how** (→ the way 또는 **how** 둘 중 하나 삭제) I could get in touch with Jiseok. He gave me Jiseok's cell phone number.

4 Tomorrow, I will call Jiseok, **that (→ who)** was my good friend when I was young.

해석

나의 어린 시절 친구

1 나는 지난 토요일에 조용하고 아름다운 어딘가를 방문했다. 내가 방문한 장소는 나의 고향이었다. 내가 거기에 방문한 이유는 나의 어린 시절을 기억하기

위해서이다.

2 나는 아들의 이름이 지석인 한 할아버지를 만났다. 그는 내가 어렸을 때 나의 친구들 중 한 명이었다.

3 나는 지석과 함께 놀았던 많은 시간을 기억한다. 내가 서울로 이사한 이후로 우리는 연락이 끊어졌다. 나는 그 할아버지에게 지석과 연락할 방법을 물었다. 그는 나에게 지석의 휴대전화 번호를 주었다.

4 내일 나는 내가 어렸을 적에 나의 좋은 친구였던 지석에게 전화할 것이다.

Paragraph Writing   p.38

Model Answer

A White Dog

1 Last week, a cute puppy, whose color is white came into my house. My younger sister who is an elementary school student told me to raise the puppy in our house.

2 My house is the place where pets can't live. The reason why no pets are in my house is my dad doesn't like animals. The reason (why) he hates animals is that he was bitten by a fierce dog when he was young.

3 It was different for raising dogs when he was bitten by the dog. Most people raised dogs in their front yard. However, people raise dogs in the houses these days. My sister and I are supposed to go to an animal shelter with my dad. That might be the only way he gets interested in animals.

4 What I want my dad to do after visiting the animal shelter is for him to allow us to raise the white dog.

Chapter **4**

to부정사와 동명사

UNIT 07 to부정사와 동명사의 쓰임 ① 주어, 보어

Simple Test

p.40

1 To express
2 of
3 for
4 sending

Practice Test

p.41

1 Beginning something on time is very important.
2 Your duty is to wash ten cars a day.
3 My older brother's dream is being a great doctor.
4 To learn new information is to broaden your knowledge.
5 It was very careless of the boy to break the window.
6 It is natural for immigrants to experience culture shock.
7 Buying her one hundred flowers will make her happy.
8 Raising your hand in the class will make you overcome fear.
9 Not giving water to the puppies is very cruel.
10 It is very brave of him to protect her in front of many (= a lot of = lots of) people.

Actual Test

p.42

1 Being [To be] patient for a long time can create a better result.
2 Did you hear about their coming back to Seoul last week?
3 I really appreciate his visiting my parents yesterday.
4 It is very annoying for the naughty children to follow me.
5 Remembering patriots is very important for teaching people about their history.
6 Today's very important duty is to rescue the shipwrecked sailors quickly.
7 What she cannot do this weekend is (to) attend the family gathering.
8 It is very kind of him not to tell everyone her weak point.
9 It is effective for brain development for children to eat nuts every day.
10 It was very brave of him to bring the child out of the raging fire.

UNIT 08 to 부정사와 동명사의 쓰임 ② 목적어

Simple Test

p.43

1 to pass
2 making
3 eating

Practice Test

p.44

1 That small cat wanted to eat a big fish.
2 He enjoys playing golf on weekends.
3 She remembered to go to the museum this afternoon.
4 The critics finally stopped arguing with each other [one another].
5 The long distance runner didn't (= did not) give up finishing the full marathon.
6 Many high school students hate studying math over two hours a day.
7 She stopped to buy fresh fruits in front of the grocery store.
8 Students continued finding out (= to find out) the password of the school's Wi-Fi.
9 Jack forgot donating a lot of (= lots of) money last year.
10 Do I have to deny accepting his proposal?

Actual Test

p.45

1 Would you mind putting my bag in your office for a while?
2 Mom often forgets to turn off the gas stove. (= Mom often forgets to turn the gas stove off.)
3 The rat [mouse] tried to find a small hole to avoid the cat.
4 I remember having a good time with my hometown friends last year.
5 The children avoided watching horror movies.
6 She minded having the public know about her private life.
7 We needed to leave the city in a hurry because of the storm.
8 My grandparents enjoy living in the country with their old friends.
9 On the sofa, she finished sending an email with her laptop computer.
10 They suddenly delayed holding a big conference next month.

Correcting Errors ❶

p.46

1 Can you **finish making** the cake in two hours?
2 To solve these problems **is** not easy for me.
3 Today's duty is **to feed** the fish in the aquarium.
4 Don't give up **memorizing** the numbers even if it seems difficult.
5 She'll never forget **travelling [traveling]** across Europe.
6 You have to stop **eating** fast food for your health.
7 They really wanted **to experience** the joy of adventure.
8 It is very nice **of** her to help the children.

Correcting Errors ❷

p.47

Playing Badminton

1 **Play** (→ **Playing**) badminton is very good for your health. I play it every Sunday.
2 My father is one of my best friends. He helps me to play it well. It is very nice **for** (→ **of**) him to help me.
3 I remember **to learn** (→ **learning**) badminton for the first time when I was 8 years old. We enjoyed **to play** (→ **playing**) it together. I was poor at playing it, but my father didn't give up **to teach** (→ **teaching**) me. Thanks to my father, I learned **playing** (→ **to play**) it very well. **Be** (→ **Being**) healthy is very important. I am trying to lose weight by playing badminton.
4 Now, I am very good at playing badminton. Do you want **playing** (→ **to play**) badminton with me? You will be much healthier if you play badminton.

해석

배드민턴 치기

1 배드민턴을 치는 것은 네 건강에 매우 좋다. 너는 매주 일요일에 배드민턴을 한다.
2 나의 아버지는 나의 가장 좋은 친구 중 한 명이다. 그는 내가 그것을 잘 하도록 도와준다. 나를 도와주는 것을 보니 그는 매우 친절하다.
3 나는 내가 8살 때 배드민턴을 처음으로 배웠던 것을 기억한다. 우리는 함께 배드민턴을 즐겼다. 나는 배드민턴을 매우 못 쳤다. 하지만 나의 아버지는 나를 가르치는 것을 포기하지 않았다. 나의 아버지 덕분에 나는 배드민턴을 치는 것을 매우 잘 배웠다. 건강한 것은 매우 중요하다. 나는 배드민턴을 함으로써 체중을 줄이는 노력을 하고 있다.
4 이제 나는 배드민턴을 매우 잘 친다. 나와 함께 배드민턴을 치기를 원하니? 만약 배드민턴을 친다면 너는 훨씬 더 건강해질 것이다.

Paragraph Writing

p.48

Model Answer

Spinners

1 Students sometimes like to play (= like playing) with spinners. My younger brother enjoys playing with a spinner.

2 I don't know who invented the spinner, but many students say that they feel relaxed when they spin a spinner. The reason why spinners are used is students who are bored with [tired of] studying may choose spinners as a way to relax.

3 It is a lot of fun to spin a spinner. I remember playing with a pinwheel when I was young. I think spinners are just like pinwheels. Spinners and pinwheels spin steadily.

4 Life is also like a spinner which spins constantly. I want to do my best tomorrow not to lose my future dream.

Chapter 5

완료시제

UNIT 09 현재완료와 과거

Simple Test
p.50

1 has been
2 visited
3 Have you eaten
4 repairing

Practice Test
p.51

1 They have already arrived in Seoul.
2 Have you ever lived in Jeju Island?
3 Have you known him for a long time?
4 He has not come back home yet.
5 The painter has just finished painting his portrait.
6 The engineers have been working hard.
7 How long have you lived in Daegu?
8 The boys have never been to the building.

9 She has been waiting for a delivery man all day long.
10 They have heard his life story for ten years.

Actual Test
p.52

1 Jaden has lived at his grandmother's house since he was young.
2 Beth has been to Africa twice.
3 We haven't finished (= have not finished) our assignment yet.
4 When did you take part in the contest?
5 We have been good friends with each other [one another] for over ten years.
6 My older brother has already left for Seoul for another audition.
7 The miners have been mining coal at the mine for five hours.
8 We have not been saving money for our vacation.
9 Have you (ever) experienced culture shock in another country?
10 Some politicians have thrown away their conscience because they have taken bribes. (= Because some politicians have taken bribes, they have thrown away their conscience.)

UNIT 10 과거완료와 미래완료

Simple Test
p.53

1 will have arrived
2 had closed
3 will have been
4 sends

Practice Test
p.54

1 The deer had been alive until then.
2 He had been to Tokyo before.
3 I had never spoken English to foreigners until then.

4 I lost my new glasses which I had bought last week.

5 When she called me, I had already submitted my report. (= I had already submitted my report when she called me.)

6 Before it rained, he had already washed his car. (= He had already washed his car before it rained.)

7 When I sent an email, he had already left his office. (= He had already left his office when I sent an email.)

8 If Sean goes to Canada again, he will have been there five times. (= Sean will have been there five times if he goes to Canada again.)

9 I will have run this restaurant for a year by next month.

10 By the time you come back, I will have fixed your computer. (= I will have fixed your computer by the time you come back.)

Actual Test

p.55

1 She told me (that) he had already cleaned the room.

2 When an ambulance arrived there, people had already disappeared.
(= People had already disappeared when an ambulance arrived there.)

3 The construction workers will not have demolished the house by next year.

4 I will have lived in Seoul for 20 years by next year.

5 When I went to the kitchen, my mom had already finished preparing dinner. (= My mom had already finished preparing dinner when I went to the kitchen.)

6 When the rich merchant sent money, she had already been at the bank. (= She had already been at the bank when the rich merchant sent money.)

7 Jina will have been in the hospital for two months by next Sunday.

8 When they arrived at the concert hall, the tickets had already sold out. (= The tickets had already sold out when they arrived at the concert hall.)

9 My grandparents will have been married for 50 years by next year.

10 When I came home, someone had already eaten my chicken. (= Someone had already eaten my chicken when I came home.)

Correcting Errors ❶

p.56

1 Jack **finished** his project yesterday.

2 Have you ever **been to** France?

3 When his mom came back home, he **had** already cleaned his room.

4 I **will have lived** in Seoul for 15 years if I stay for one more month.

5 When **did** you call Jane?

6 They **have been waiting** for the singer since morning.

7 My younger brother **had** already removed the file when I entered the room.

8 If he goes again, he **will have been** Jeju Island three times.

Correcting Errors ❷

p.57

Art Museum

1 I **have** (삭제) visited an art museum with my friends yesterday. The art museum will have **open** (→ **been open**) for 20 year by next month.

2 The museum **collects** (→ **had collected**) a lot of paintings before a new museum was needed. The city wants to collect even more paintings but this is too small.

3 Many people **has asked** (→ **have asked**) the city to build a new art museum for a long time. So, the mayor of the city has just decided to build a new art museum.

4 The art museum has long opening hours and is free to the public. I had great time with my friends there.

미술관

1 나는 어제 나의 친구들과 미술관을 방문했다. 그 미술관은 다음 달이면 문을 연 지 20년이 되는 셈이다.

2 그 미술관은 새로운 미술관이 필요로 하기 전에 많은 그림을 수집해왔다. 도시는 훨씬 더 많은 그림을 수집하기를 원하는데 이곳은 너무 작다.

3 많은 사람이 새로운 미술관을 건설하자고 오랫동안 도시에 요청해왔다. 그래서 그 도시의 시장은 새로운 미술관을 건설할 것을 방금 결정했다.

4 그 미술관은 문을 여는 시간이 길고, 대중들에게 무료이다. 나는 나의 친구들과 그곳에서 좋은 시간을 가졌다.

Paragraph Writing
p.58

Model Answer

Traveling overseas

1 I have never traveled overseas. Before my friend Daniel told me about his trips, I had not been interested in traveling. (= I had not been interested in traveling before my friend Daniel told me about his trips.)

2 He has been to Japan and China only once, and he has been to America twice. He will have been to Europe by next year. Recently, he let me know the pleasures he gets from traveling.

3 But he told me (that) he had to prepare some money for his next trip. I thought Daniel had prepared a lot. I had saved a lot of money in the bank for 5 years.

4 I will have traveled by myself next year, and I will have had a good time with my friend Daniel in Europe by next summer.

Chapter **6**

수동태

UNIT 11 단순형 수동태

Simple Test
p.60

1 at

2 was frozen

3 to wash

Practice Test
p.61

1 The professor was very satisfied with Tim's thesis.

2 His novel is known to many (= a lot of = lots of) people.

3 The letter was sent to Spain yesterday.

4 English is spoken in many (= a lot of = lots of) countries.

5 Max was raised by his grandmother.

6 The masterpiece was created by a talented artist.

7 The girl was hit on her back by a fast ball.

8 The old broken clock was repaired yesterday.

9 The fly was killed by that bug spray.

10 The old man was interested in finding wild ginseng.

Actual Test
p.62

1 This old piece of pottery was made 500 years ago.

2 They were caught in heavy rain on their way home.

3 His messy room was cleaned up by his sister.

4 Molly was made by her mom to buy some eggs.

5 Julia was seen by many (= a lot of = lots of) friends to play the guitar on the stage.

6 I was told that a beautiful rainbow came out over the river.

7 It is shocking that a lot of (= lots of) news is written untruthfully.

8 The child was given some chocolate by the man.

9 I was advised by my English teacher to memorize ten vocabulary words a day.

10 The car salesman was made by his boss to sell ten cars a month.

 **UNIT 12 복합형 수동태**

Simple Test
p.63

1 to be delayed
2 is said
3 will be sent

Practice Test
p.64

1 He is required to attend the weekly meeting.
2 Nobody can be allowed to enter here.
3 He advised me to relax more often.
4 Onions are said to be good for health.
5 The child was being protected by a brave man.
6 She is obliged to have a medical check-up once a month.
7 The festival was taken part in by them because of James' invitation.
8 She will be recruited by a top-ranked global company.
9 He will be given a prize thanks to good marks.
10 It is said that smartphones are not good for communication.

Actual Test
p.65

1 The guests are scheduled to visit a traditional restaurant this evening.
2 Unnecessary files were got(ten) rid of by the staff this afternoon.
3 Their desire was being served with fresh food.
4 It is said that milk is good for overcoming of insomnia.

5 This airplane was supposed to arrive in Hong Kong.
6 Being traded to other team is very disappointing for athletes.
7 It is said that real freedom is loving each other [one another].
8 James is said to be considerate of others all the time.
9 The fact that the company is hiding something should be known to the public.
10 We hope (that) the important documents are to be sent to the lawyer as soon as possible.

Correcting Errors **I**
p.66

1 They were satisfied **with** the final score.
2 The patient was made **to take** the medicine every day by the doctor.
3 He was **interested** in collecting toy cars.
4 The report should **be submitted** by tomorrow.
5 This marble can **be seen** in the dark because it glows.
6 It is said **that** walnuts are good for the brains.
7 He wanted the packages **to be sent** to Canada.
8 Some trash **was got(ten) rid of** from the street.

Correcting Errors **II**
p.67

The Importance of Preparation

1 I **am** (추가) supposed to meet some potential new clients tomorrow. Being **chose** (→ **chosen**) by new clients is very exciting.
2 It **is** (추가) said that preparing well is very important to attracting people's attention.
3 I have a lot of things to prepare for tomorrow's meeting. I am interested **at** (→ **in**) making a good presentation. An effective presentation will be **show** (→ **shown**) to the clients. There will be over five people who

14

will compete for this business.

4 However, I am sure that my suggestions will be (추가) selected. I want the clients to be **satisfying** (→ **satisfied**). I think that preparing hard makes someone a winner. Why don't you prepare to win?

해석

준비의 중요성

1 나는 내일 몇몇 새로운 잠재 신규 의뢰인을 만나기로 되어 있다. 새로운 의뢰인에 의해 선택받는 것은 매우 흥미롭다.

2 준비를 잘하는 것은 사람들의 주의를 끄는 데에 매우 중요하다고들 한다.

3 나는 내일 회의에 준비해야 할 많은 것들이 있다. 나는 좋은 프레젠테이션을 만드는 것에 흥미가 있다. 효과적인 프레젠테이션이 의뢰인들에게 보일 것이다. 이 사업에 경쟁할 사람은 5명을 넘을 것이다.

4 그러나, 나는 나의 제안이 선택될 것이라고 확신한다. 나는 의뢰인들이 만족하기를 원한다. 나는 열심히 준비하는 것은 누군가를 승리자가 되게 한다고 생각한다. 이기기 위해 준비를 하는 것이 어때?

Paragraph Writing
p.68

Model Answer

War and Peace

1 My grandfather told me about the Korean War yesterday. In 1950, South Korea was attacked by North Korea suddenly one Sunday at dawn, and many people had to flee.

2 Some tall friends of my grandfather were quickly sent to fight. My grandfather was short, so he wasn't sent to fight. Many friends of my grandfather were killed in battles. It was terrible.

3 It is said that war should not be allowed to occur again. (= War is said not to be allowed to occur again. = They said war should not be allowed to occur again.) I think that peace should be spread everywhere in the world. All people should be united for peace.

4 So, I try to keep good relationships with my friends. This will be the first step toward peace.

Chapter **7**

분사

UNIT 13 현재분사와 과거분사

Simple Test
p.70

1 rising
2 boring
3 annoyed

Practice Test
p.71

1 The irritated boy ran home rapidly.
2 A small paper ship is floating on the water.
3 I bought a very exciting novel this afternoon.
4 They were watering the trees on the rooftop of the building.
5 My father brought home an abandoned dog on the street.
6 Jeremy's report is brief, but it is very satisfying.
7 Humiliating punishments are not desirable for students.
8 Look at the squirrel jumping and trying to climb the tree. (= Look at the jumping squirrel trying to climb the tree.)
9 Let's put the littered cans on the ground in the recycling bin.
10 Let sleeping dogs alone.

Actual Test
p.72

1 Why don't you love all living creatures?

2 All the candidates wanted people to be satisfied.

3 I was interested in drawing characters when I was young. (= When I was young, I was interested in drawing characters.)

4 The situation was confusing, so we were very confused.

5 The two boys were frightened in the dark forest last night.

6 Many surprising things happened to me last summer.

7 "The Treasure Hunt" excited many children, and they were pleased.

8 There are five very annoying boys in Sally's class.

9 David encouraged the frustrated students sincerely.

10 I am very depressed because the baseball team that I support lost the game today. (= Because the baseball team that I support lost the game today, I am very depressed.)

UNIT 14 분사구문

Practice Test
p.74

1 Listening to music, Michael was waiting for a bus.

2 Holding his new cell phone, Jihun fell asleep.

3 Getting my first paycheck, I will buy a new laptop (computer).

4 Calling someone, the bank teller counted the money.

5 Being too young, he can't take a bus by himself.

6 Not being hungry, the lions just took a nap.

7 Finishing a piece of pizza, he brushed his teeth.

8 Not being late for school, he had enough time to have breakfast.

9 Losing many (= a lot of = lots of) soldiers,

they couldn't fight anymore.

10 He being very rude, the teacher called his mother immediately.

Actual Test
p.75

1 Attending the conference, you will get a lot of (= lots of) information.

2 The train having departed, they had to wait for the next train.

3 She went home with Teddy waiting for her on the street.

4 The boy got on the bus with his backpack slung over his shoulder.

5 He having watered the flowers regularly, they are blooming now.

6 You opening a new shop at the beach, many (= a lot of = lots of) friends will visit there.

7 Not having exercised at all, Steve felt tired easily and lacked energy.

8 They not finding a new solution, he called a meeting in the afternoon.

9 Not having enough money, they couldn't send their son to Germany.

10 The boss not giving him another chance, his team members went to talk to the boss. (= The boss not giving another chance to him, his team members went to talk to the boss.)

Correcting Errors 1
p.76

1 Can you repair the **broken** machine as soon as possible?

2 The story that you sent yesterday was very **touching**.

3 The food at the new restaurant is **disappointing**.

4 The passengers were **annoyed** because of the flight delay.

5 While **flying** the kite to the sky, the boy called his friends.

6 **Turning right**, you can find a public library.

7 **Having studied** too much, she took a rest for a while.

8 **Not understanding** their language, he looked up the dictionary.

The Reason for Different Price

1 There are two stores selling this wine. The price **been** (→ **being**) different between two stores, many people wonder about the wine's quality. **Sold** (→ **Selling**) the same product, they should have set the same price.

2 But store A's wine is much cheaper than store B's. **Reduced** (→ **Reducing**) the costs of distribution, store A can sell cheaper wine.

3 The quality is the same. The problem is the process. **Reducing not** (→ **Not reducing**) the costs of distribution, store B has to sell the wine to consumers at a more expensive price than store B.

4 Which store do you want to buy from?

해석

가격이 다른 이유

1 이 와인을 파는 두 가게가 있다. 두 가게 사이에 가격이 다르기 때문에 많은 사람들이 와인의 품질에 대해 궁금해한다. 똑같은 제품을 판매하기 때문에 그들은 같은 가격을 정해야 했다.

2 그러나 A 가게의 와인은 B 가게의 것보다 훨씬 더 저렴하다. 유통비용을 줄이기 때문에 A 가게는 더 저렴한 와인을 판매할 수 있다.

3 품질은 같다. 문제는 과정이다. 유통비용을 줄이지 않기 때문에 B 가게는 소비자들에게 B 가게보다 더 비싼 가격으로 와인을 팔아야 한다.

4 너는 어느 가게에서 사기를 원하니?

Paragraph Writing p.78

Model Answer

Genius Troublemakers

1 Having a lot of (= lots of) curiosity, Thomas Edison did a lot of (= lots of = many) special things when he was young. Sitting on eggs to see chicks hatch is one of his famous episodes.

2 The result of his experiments being disappointing, he planned more experiments. Bothering [Upsetting, Annoying] a lot of (= lots of = many) people, he was called a troublemaker.

3 Henry Ford who was the founder of Ford Motor Company was also a troublemaker when he was young. He was born 16 years later than Edison.

4 One day, being invited to a dinner party at Edison's, he asked some questions of Edison. Edison having given him good advice, Henry Ford could found "Ford Motor Company". Encouraged by Edison, Ford continued to build [make] vehicles.

Chapter 8

가정법

UNIT 15 가정법 과거와 가정법 과거완료

Simple Test p.80

1 ran
2 were
3 had not been
4 have been
5 have had

Practice Test p.81

1 If I were you, I would sell the car right now.
(= I would sell the car right now if I were

you.)

2 If he were not selfish, many people would like him. (= Many people would like him if he were not selfish.)

3 If I were a famous singer, I would have many (= a lot of = lots of) concerts. (= I would have many (= a lot of = lots of) concerts if I were a famous singer.)

4 If the wise woman were my girlfriend, I would be happy. (= I would be happy if the wise woman were my girlfriend.)

5 If he had not drunken a lot of coffee, he could have gone to bed early. (= He could have gone to bed early if he had not drunken a lot of coffee.)

6 If the deer had not been hungry, it wouldn't have been caught in the trap. (= The deer wouldn't have been caught in the trap if it had not been hungry.)

7 If he hadn't had much money, they wouldn't have deceived him. (= They wouldn't have deceived him if he hadn't had much money.)

8 If Tony had liked reading books then, he would have already read the book. (= Tony would have already read the book if he had liked reading books then.)

9 If I had had my own car, I could have taken her to the party. (= I could have taken her to the party if I had had my own car.)

10 If she knew about computers well, she could fix her broken computer. (= She could fix her broken computer if she knew about computers well.)

Actual Test

p.82

1 If it were raining now, the fine dust would disappear. (= The fine dust would disappear if it were raining now.)

2 If they solved this crisis, they would be much stronger. (= They would be much stronger if they solved this crisis.)

3 If he had had the medicine, he could have recovered faster. (= He could have recovered faster if he had had the medicine.)

4 If they had fastened their seat belts, they wouldn't have been badly hurt in the accident. (= They wouldn't have been badly hurt in the accident if they had fastened their seat belts.)

5 If there weren't soccer to play, the boys would be bored in their free time. (= The boys would be bored in their free time if there weren't soccer to play.)

6 If he hadn't submitted the report, many people would have worked overtime tonight. (= Many people would have worked overtime tonight if he hadn't submitted the report.)

7 If I were good at drawing, I could draw her portrait. (= I could draw her portrait if I were good at drawing.)

8 If she liked bread, the baker would give her a lot of bread. (= If she liked bread, the baker would give a lot of bread to her. = The baker would give her a lot of bread if she liked bread. = The baker would give a lot of bread to her if she liked bread.)

9 If there had not been a traffic jam, we could have reached our destination on time. (= We could have reached our destination on time, if there had not been a traffic jam.)

10 If there had not been any convenience stores in our neighborhood, we couldn't have bought milk late last night. (= We couldn't have bought milk late last night if there had not been any convenience stores in our neighborhood.)

UNIT 16 여러 가지 가정법

Practice Test

p.84

1 I wish (that) I were a cartoonist.
2 I wish (that) I were in the Maldives.
3 She talks as if she knew everything.
4 Without movies, my life would be boring.
5 I wish (that) I had called my grandmother more.

6 But for coffee, I would feel sleepy every day.

7 Steve talks as if he were a tennis player.

8 He always talks as if he were good at singing.

9 If it were not for love, people would not be happy. (= People would not be happy if it were not for love.)

10 I wish (that) bad people in the world would disappear.

Actual Test
p.85

1 I wish (that) I had spent more time with the poor children.

2 He smiled as if he had known the answer.

3 I wished (that) everybody were satisfied with the result.

4 She shouted loudly as though she were frightened.

5 He looked happy as if he had got a job in a good company.

6 The doctor wished (that) all diseases in the world would not exist.

7 Were it not for his leadership, we could not have escaped from the serious situation.

8 But for the fireman's help, Philip would not have survived the accident.

9 She knows many stories as though she had watched all the dramas. (= As though she had watched all the dramas, she knows many stories.)

10 Were it not for cell phones, many (= a lot of = lots of) teenagers could communicate more.

Correcting Errors ❶
p.86

1 If I **were** you, I would apply for the company.

2 If he had a lot of time, he **could** prepare the report much better.

3 If they had had a lot of money, they **could have bought** that building.

4 If the policeman **had been** in the bank, he could have caught the thief.

5 I wish that I **could** compose beautiful songs.

6 I wish I **had had breakfast** before the meeting this morning.

7 Sarah talks as if she **knew** everything about her.

8 **If** it were not for the navigation systems, we couldn't drive conveniently. (= **Were it not for [But for, Without]** the navigation systems, we couldn't drive conveniently.)

Correcting Errors ❶❶
p.87

I wish ...

1 Hi, my name is John. I live in Korea. I have a dream. I really want to speak English well. I wish I **was** (→ **had been**) born in Canada.

2 If I **am** (→ **were**) living in Canada, I would speak English very well. My younger brother Sam usually talks as if he **speaks** (→ **could speak**) English very well. But I know how poor his spoken English is.

3 **But with** (→ **But for**) an English dictionary, I could not speak and write English well. I would like to speak English well. So every day I will repeat many times five English expressions. I think that going to Canada is a good way to speak English better.

4 I wish I could **lived** (→ **live**) in beautiful Canada. If you get a chance to go there, please take me with you!

해석

좋을 텐데 ...

1 안녕, 나의 이름은 John이야. 나는 대한민국에 살아. 나는 꿈이 있어. 나는 영어를 정말 잘하고 싶어. 내가 캐나다에서 태어났으면 좋을 텐데…

2 만약 내가 캐나다에 살고 있다면 나는 영어를 잘 말할 수 있을 텐데. 나의 남동생 Sam은 주로 그가 영어를 매우 잘 말할 수 있는 것처럼 말한다. 그러나 나는 그의 영어회화가 얼마나 형편없는지 알고 있다.

3 영어사전이 없다면 나는 영어를 잘 말하거나 쓸 수 없다. 나는 영어를 잘 말하고 싶다. 그래서 나는 매일 5가지의 영어표현들을 여러 번 반복할 것이다. 나는 캐나다에 가는 것이 영어를 더 잘 말할 수 있는 좋은 방법이라고

생각한다.

4 내가 아름다운 캐나다에서 살면 좋을 텐데. 만약 네가 거기에 갈 기회가 생긴다면 부디 나를 너와 함께 데려가 줘.

Paragraph Writing   p.88

Model Answer

My Bowling Club

1 I like going bowling. I am one of the bowling club members in this city. There are many (= a lot of = lots of) people in my bowling club. Let me introduce some friends to you.

2 Tom! He always talks as if he had been a professional bowler when he was younger. I think if he showed us some videos and photos, he could prove it. Kevin! If I were Kevin, I would enter many (= a lot of = lots of) bowling competitions. He bowls very well. Ben! But for (= Without = If it were not for) his long practices, he could not score over 200 points. He practices every day as if he were a professional player. Terry! He is poor at bowling. Every time he bowls it is as if he had never bowled before.

3 Whenever I bowl, I just want to enjoy it. (= I just want to enjoy it whenever I bowl.) Were it not for (= Without = But for) bowling, I would not be happy.

Chapter 9

주요 구문

UNIT 17 비교 구문

Simple Test   p.90

1 interesting

2 possible

3 the healthier

4 am

Practice Test   p.91

1 The park isn't (= is not) as[so] big as I expected.

2 They finished the investigation as quickly as possible.

3 He is not (= isn't) a doctor but a nurse.

4 Everything got better and better.

5 Either you or Carl has to go there.

6 Not only you but (also) I can't drink any water because of the health check-ups.

7 They used a fan as well as an air conditioner.

8 This building is the oldest of all these buildings.

9 Both police officers and firefighters rescued them safely.

10 The cooler it is, the more often people go on picnics.

Actual Test   p.92

1 The more you understand, the better the world will be.

2 The more positive we are, the happier we become.

3 Environmental pollution is getting more serious these days.

4 Not I but she is interested in underwater exploration.

5 The boa constrictor is the most threatening animal in the jungle.

6 James is the most challenging and faithful boy of the students.

7 The committee is neither conservative nor progressive.

8 The surgeon is as careful as a Baduk player.

9 They had a funeral for the dog as quietly as possible.

10 Illegal hunting as well as global warming is an important global issue.

UNIT 18 강조, 도치, 동격 구문

Practice Test

p.94

1 Under the tree took a nap the rabbit.
2 Rarely does my nephew eat vegetables.
3 The king himself gave the letter to him.
4 On the branch was the beautiful bird twittering.
5 It was last week that [when] they gave an impressive concert.
6 It was in front of the Japanese Embassy that [where] he met her yesterday.
7 Never did he expect to pass the test.
8 The fact that he separated from his wife is shocking.
9 They started a blog so that they can communicate with more people.
10 He did share his whole fortune with poor people (= the poor).

Actual Test

p.95

1 The belief that he would be hired came true.
2 Assessments themselves cannot (= can't) be changed.
3 It was Jacob that [who] they recommended for mayor.
4 They classified books in order that the library could be relocated.
5 Every morning he plays tennis to keep fit.
6 Little did she think about tomorrow's assignment.
7 The thought that the teacher was indifferent to students was wrong.
8 He did spend a lot of (= lots of) money on buying new shoes.
9 It was at the bus stop that [where] he lost his wallet this morning.
10 She visited many (= a lot of = lots of) stores so that she could buy old furniture for her collection.

Correcting Errors I

p.96

1 The new smartphone is as innovative **as** the laptop.
2 The scientists wanted to invent the machine as soon as **possible**.
3 The more water we drink, **the healthier** we will get.
4 The boy as well as I **has** to arrive there on time.
5 It was at the bus stop **that [where]** I first met her last year.
6 He does **like** to go fishing on weekends.
7 Never **does my dad give** me money for buying concert tickets.
8 At that time, several people didn't accept the fact **that** the Earth is round.

Correcting Errors II

p.97

The Huge Animal

1 In the jungle were there many animals. In the trees **some sleeping monkeys were**. (→ **were some sleeping monkeys**.) In the pond **some scary alligators were**. (→ **were some scary alligators**.)
2 One day, a huge animal appeared. Its size was as **bigger** (→ **big**) as an elephant. **Never had seen the animals in the jungle** (→ **Never had the animals in the jungle seen**) such a big animal. Monkeys as well as alligators **was** (→ **were**) scared.
3 It was the biggest animal in the jungle. More and **many** (→ **more**) animals gathered to see the huge animal. One of them shouted. "It's not moving. It is not only not moving **so** (→ **but (also)**) not breathing!"
4 One of the brave monkeys shouted again. "It's not an animal but ~~also~~ (삭제) a huge tent that men have set up for studying our jungle."

거대한 동물

1 정글에는 많은 동물들이 있었다. 나무에는 몇몇 잠자는 원숭이들이 있었다. 연못에는 몇몇 무서운 악어들이 있었다.

2 어느 날, 한 거대한 동물이 나타났다. 그것의 크기는 코끼리만큼 컸다. 그 정글에 있는 동물들은 그렇게 큰 동물을 본 적이 없었다. 악어들뿐만 아니라 원숭이들도 겁을 먹었다.

3 그것은 정글에서 가장 큰 동물이었다. 점점 더 많은 동물들이 그 거대한 동물을 보기 위해 모였다. 그들 중 하나가 소리쳤다. "그것은 움직이지 않아요. 움직이지 않을 뿐 아니라 숨도 쉬지 않아요."

4 원숭이 중 가장 용감한 한 마리가 다시 소리쳤다. "그것은 동물이 아니라 사람이 우리의 정글을 연구하기 위해 설치한 텐트야."

Paragraph Writing
p.98

Model Answer

My First Presentation

1 I had a presentation last week. It was the first presentation in my life. In the library read I a lot of (= lots of = many) books. The more books I read, the more comfortable I was.

2 It was my father that [who] I asked for some advice for the presentation. In his company gives my father many (= a lot of = lots of) presentations.

3 I needed not only a good script but (also) good presentation skills. So I saw as many videos as possible to give a good presentation and practiced every day. Finally, I did give a good presentation. After my presentation, many (= a lot of = lots of) teachers and students clapped. I will practice more so that I will give a better presentation next time. That's because now I have changed my dream into being an excellent announcer.

4 Never did I expect that I would want to be an announcer before my first presentation. You can prepare wonderful presentations and give them well, too. It's not difficult.

Final Test 1
p.100

1 They helped her to arrive at the city safely.

2 I don't know whether [if] they are our enemies or not.

3 She minded visiting strange cities by herself.

4 My family will have lived here for 20 years next year.

5 Joy doesn't remember the city where [in which] she was born.

6 These cans will be thrown away.

7 Her room was filled with a good smell.

8 He did memorize hundreds of words.

9 It was at the hospital that the baby was crying.

10 Being tall, he was good at playing basketball.

11 He couldn't remember going to Busan last summer.

12 Not doing anything in the amusement park is very unusual.

13 They have been making some cards since yesterday.

14 Never did I dream that he had left here.

15 I didn't know what they told her.

16 It is said that lobsters are delicious.

17 He bought a good bicycle [bike] for Steve.

18 As soon as he got home, he drank a cup of cold water.

19 Not knowing his address, I couldn't send it to his friend Tom.

20 If he had not been sick, he would have finished his homework.

Final Test 2
p.102

1 The girl and the puppy that are running in the park live next door to me.

2 What I really want to do is traveling for a year.

3 As long as he stays here, I will help him. (= I will help him as long as he stays here.)

4 They worked over 10 hours today so that

they can succeed.

5 You are supposed to take care of those children today.

6 Being promoted is a good thing for everyone.

7 We must not forget the place (where) many (= a lot of = lots of) people were sacrificed.

8 I had dinner with her whose father is a famous movie star.

9 It is very kind of him to help the elderly every day.

10 Don't forget to close the windows before going out.

11 He entered the office, and read the newspaper.

12 The question made many (= a lot of = lots of) students confused.

13 When he went to the bank, it had already closed. (= It had already closed when he went to the bank.)

14 When I get home, my son will have fallen asleep. (= My son will have fallen asleep when I get home.)

15 The movie was very exciting, so we were satisfied.

16 Billy being polite, many (= a lot of = lots of) teachers like him.

17 If I had two apples, I would give you one. (= If I had two apples, I would give one to you. = I would give you one if I had two apples. = I would give one to you if I had two apples.)

18 He talks as if he could walk on water.

19 Neither I nor she is good at playing golf.

20 It was in this park that he first learned how to ride a bicycle [bike].

MEMO

제대로
영작문
5

서술형·수행평가 만점을 만드는 좋은 영작 습관!

제대로 영작문

4 정답

DARAKWON

제대로 영작문

4 완성

DARAKWON

Chapter 1

완료

 UNIT 01 현재완료와 과거완료

Simple Test

p.10

1 Have you ever been to Texas?
2 When I called her, she had already left Seoul.
3 Had you ordered the new product before he called?
4 They had stayed in the island for one week before the accident.

Practice Test

p.11

1 He had worked for twelve hours by midnight yesterday.
2 The captain had escaped from the ship before the rescue ship arrived.
3 Has Paul ever used a compass before?
4 I had already finished writing the report before I went for lunch. (= I had already finished writing the report before going for lunch.)
5 He has been the coach of the soccer team for the last two years.
6 When I arrived at the stadium, the game had already started. (= The game had already started when I arrived at the stadium.)
7 I knew (that) she had been a famous consultant for a long time.
8 There had been a big flood in this town before I moved here.
9 When I stopped by the restaurant, it had already closed. (= It had already closed when I stopped by the restaurant.)

10 Jiyu has just finished the musical concert at her school.

Actual Test

p.12

1 The general has worked in the unit for five years.
2 When Jihun opened the refrigerator, the milk in the bottle had gone bad. (= The milk in the bottle had gone bad when Jihun opened the refrigerator.)
3 She has taught both art and music for a long time.
4 I had confessed my love to her before Paul did it.
5 He has used a fan instead of air conditioning for ten years.
6 The group has recently been reunited.
7 She had never prayed before she was in the crisis.
8 Nobody had visited the town before then.
9 Since she graduated from university, she hasn't found a job. (= She hasn't found a job since she graduated from university.)
10 Some of you have helped poor people (= the poor), and others haven't.

 UNIT 02 미래완료, 완료 진행형

Simple Test

p.13

1 I will have repaired his car by Saturday.
2 They will have been married for seven years by next month.
3 They have been looking for her for an hour.

Practice Test

p.14

1 He will have donated a thousand dollars by the end of this year.
2 She will have reserved two plane tickets to Paris when we meet later today. (= When we meet later today, she will have reserved two plane tickets.)

3 He has been waiting for her for seven hours.

4 She has always thought of him as someone to trust.

5 Mom will have cooked dinner when we get home. (= When we get home, Mom will have cooked dinner.)

6 By next year, I will have been a fan of the soccer team for five years.

7 Tom was a little tired because he had been working hard on his homework. (= Because he had been working hard on his homework, Tom was a little tired.)

8 He has been texting her for three hours.

9 I will have packed all my stuff by the time the truck arrives. (= By the time the truck arrives, I will have packed all my stuff.)

10 I will have stayed on this plane for 13 hours by ten o'clock tonight.

Actual Test
p.15

1 He has been running on the treadmill for two hours.

2 The cicada has been trying to molt all day (long).

3 He will have repaired my car by Sunday.

4 Had you been studying when she called?

5 He has been studying in the library since the exam started (= began).

6 The company has been losing money recently.

7 They have been selling flowers at the same shop for over 30 years.

8 He has been weeping all day since she left in the morning. (= Since she left in the morning, he has been weeping all day.)

9 I will have played computer games every day for seven days by tomorrow.

10 I had been sleeping for two hours when she came home. (= When she came home, I had been sleeping for two hours.)

Paragraph Writing
p.17

Model Answer

After Watching the Movie *Forrest Gump*

1 The movie *Forrest Gump* that Steven Spielberg directed and Tom Hanks starred in is a beautiful story. **I have been fond of Tom Hanks' movies for a long time.** His movies are excellent. *Forrest Gump* is regarded as one of his best movies.

2 Even though [Although, Though] his IQ was just 75, Forrest could go to school thanks to his strong mother's effort. (= Forrest could go to school thanks to his strong mother's effort even though [although, though] his IQ was just 75.) However, children teased and ignored him. Meanwhile, he met a girl whose name was Jenny, and he fell in love with her. His love for Jenny lasted until he became an adult.

3 Forrest who was really good at running was selected to be a football player on his school team. When he was in the Army, he played table tennis. (= He played table tennis when he was in the Army.) He practiced a lot until he became a great table tennis player. **In the Vietnam War, he met Bubba who had been a shrimp catcher before joining the army.** He also met Lieutenant Dan. **After the war, he made an effort to keep the promises which he had made during the war.**

4 Finally, Forrest kept all the promises and married Jenny. However, his happiness was short because she died from a disease. **After she died, he lived with his son to whom Jenny had given birth.**

5 The words that came to my mind after watching this movie were love and promise. **I will have watched all of Tom Hanks' movies soon.** I only need to watch two more of his movies. His movies always make me feel good.

Correcting Errors p.18

1 They **have lived** in Incheon since 2020.
2 **Has** she already finished her task?
3 I **will have lived** in Toronto for ten years by next year.
4 Mom had been **washing** the dishes when I saw her.
5 He **has been playing** the computer game since this morning.
6 I **have studied** English since I was a child.
7 Jack **has known** Jenny for ten years.
8 She **has not visited** her hometown since 2022.

Chapter **2**

to부정사와 동명사

UNIT 03 to부정사

Simple Test p.20

1 She <u>seems [appears]</u> to be sick.
2 She is <u>too</u> young <u>to</u> go to school.
3 He was smart <u>enough to</u> solve the difficult question.

Practice Test p.21

1 To be frank [honest], I didn't eat anything yesterday.
2 The soup was too hot to eat fast.
3 She seems to have cried in the rain last night.
4 This water is clean enough to drink.
5 He was [got] lost yesterday. To make matters worse, he lost his cell phone.

6 He is too lazy to exercise every morning.
7 These apples are ripe enough to eat.
8 Strange to say, I eat meat in the morning.
9 The kitchen seems to be filled with smoke.
10 He seems to have lived in Brazil three years ago.

Actual Test p.22

1 The road was too dark for them to see the signs.
2 The road was so dark that they couldn't see the signs.
3 She was full enough to eat the cake.
4 She was so full that she couldn't eat the cake.
5 To begin with, open the door with this key.
6 To be sure, it will rain a lot tomorrow.
7 I seem to have lost my laptop computer.
8 It seems that I lost my laptop computer.
9 He appeared to have given the children a lot of presents. (= He appeared to have given a lot of presents to the children.)
10 It appeared that he had given the children a lot of presents. (= It appeared that he had given a lot of presents to the children.)

UNIT 04 동명사

Simple Test p.23

1 <u>On</u> seeing me, Kevin smiled at me.
2 He is afraid of <u>her</u> calling him because of his mistake.

Practice Test p.24

1 They suddenly put off holding the big event.
2 Monkeys are used to climbing trees.
3 They denied her having been to Canada.
4 We could not help laughing at that time.
5 He is far from betraying us.
6 The company considered hiring Jack because he was fluent in Japanese.

(= Because Jack was fluent in Japanese, the company considered hiring him.)

7 Jane dislikes saying hello to people.

8 On her entering the room, a fly flew away.
(= A fly flew away on her entering the room.)

9 The children went on playing in the park.

10 Sean kept watching television [TV] all day long.

Actual Test
p.25

1 He was [got] sick [tired] of eating the same meal every day.

2 She is proud of her son's having passed the exam.

3 She spent a lot of (= lots of) money buying a brand-new computer.

4 Mr. Smith is so stubborn that there is no changing his mind.

5 She avoids going out on rainy days.

6 Joe is ashamed of having lost his temper yesterday.

7 I am sure of my team's winning the game.

8 I am used to driving in this city.

9 They were busy distributing flyers on the street.

10 It is no use crying over spilt milk.

Paragraph Writing
p.27

Model Answer

Minho's Love for Soccer

1 Many people like soccer. **Minho also enjoys watching soccer games.** Whenever he watches soccer games, he feels happy.
(= He feels happy whenever he watches soccer games.)

2 **Minho spends a lot of time watching the EPL (English Premier League) on TV. Last night at 2 a.m., he was busy watching a game.** He watches games late at night in Korea because that's when EPL games are played in England.

3 The team (which [that]) Minho doesn't support won the championship last year. Minho is not a fan of the team. **He admits not cheering for them. But the team deserved to win the championship. He can't help appreciating the players' skills.**

4 Minho has been cheering for his favorite team for a long time. **He is proud of being one of the team's biggest fans. He never postpones watching their games.** Minho is looking forward to a great player who can bring new hope and success to the team. **Many players on the team were disappointed with not winning the championship several times.**

5 Minho wants his favorite team to win the championship next season. He also wants Korean players to play very well. At the start of next season, Minho will be up all night again. **He looks forward to watching all of the team's games next season.**

Correcting Errors
p.28

1 She seems **to be** interested in drawing cartoons.

2 The house is **cheap enough** to buy right now.

3 They are looking forward **to going** to the amusement park.

4 My father was **busy working** in his office.

5 He is **too** young to go abroad by himself.

6 She feels like **taking** a break to recharge her energy.

7 To **tell** the truth, she doesn't like him.

8 She couldn't help **searching** the address of the restaurant through the internet.

Chapter 3

분사

UNIT 05 현재분사와 과거분사

Simple Test   p.30

1 We call him a "walking dictionary".
2 He found a hidden card under the table.
3 The small church standing on the hill is very old.
4 The fall of the dice was amazing.
5 Joel's job is to sell used cars.

Practice Test   p.31

1 They were sad to see the destroyed city.
2 That man buying some bread is my dad.
3 Most people were very excited yesterday.
4 I can't memorize such confusing words.
5 He bought me a pair of light running shoes. (= He bought a pair of light running shoes for me.)
6 We took a rest after playing a tiring game. (= After playing a tiring game, we took a rest.)
7 The wall painted in green makes me feel comfortable.
8 Cindy was moved by her daughter's present.
9 Her book report is disappointing.
10 A rolling stone gathers no moss.

Actual Test   p.32

1 The boy teasing Becky is Michael.
2 He brings me surprising news all the time. (= He brings surprising news to me all the time.)
3 That broken mirror was Jessica's favorite (mirror).
4 This is the last chance given to you.
5 She was annoyed by (= because of) the noise from next door.
6 It was the most embarrassing moment in my life.
7 We all have hidden secrets. (= All of us have hidden secrets.)
8 Her picture taken by me yesterday is very flattering.
9 The singing birds have disappeared from my backyard.
10 We have to cross this frozen river.

UNIT 06 분사구문

Simple Test   p.33

1 Having little time, I had to catch a taxi.
2 Singing songs, I feel happy.
3 Being tired, Joyce went to bed early.

Practice Test   p.34

1 Leaving Seoul, we went to Busan.
2 Not knowing her nationality, I couldn't fill in the application.
3 Watching TV in the living room, Linda did her homework.
4 Not having brought an umbrella, Sophie was caught in the rain.
5 Not hurrying up, we missed the first train.
6 Judging from her accent, she must be from Australia.
7 Never [Not] having seen humans, the dodo birds were not afraid of us.
8 Not wearing formal clothes, they couldn't enter the banquet.
9 Having sent me a letter a long time ago, he was pleased to get my reply. (= Having sent a letter to me a long time ago, he was pleased to get my reply.)
10 There being no fork, Peter had to use chopsticks.

Actual Test   p.35

1 Considering his age, he has a baby face.
2 Cathy having made a mistake, many people felt sorry for her.

3 The vacation being over, I went back to school.

4 Running too fast, I dropped my wallet.

5 Not knowing what to do, she stayed at home.

6 Frankly [Honestly] speaking, nobody knew how to use the machine.

7 Opening the door, I saw a strange man.

8 Turning to the right, you will find the embassy.

9 Coming out of the forest, he lost his way.

10 Walking along the road, she was looking at pretty flowers.

Paragraph Writing
p.37

Model Answer
Humble Leadership

1 My uncle is the most popular doctor in Korea. He is not the official representative of Korean doctors, but he seems to represent them.

2 He hosts the best medical programs on public TV, and **there are many cooperating friends who help him. Being the best doctor, he is really humble. This is one of his best qualities. Admiring him, I try to be humble too.**

3 He doesn't order people around like a king. He serves the people. **Strictly speaking, he is a healthcare provider. But he showed his leadership skills by arranging programs to help communities that don't have enough medical services.** He wants everyone to get the medical help they need.

4 **Staying focused on helping others, he doesn't seek fame but cares for his patients and communities.** His actions show that he's not just a skilled doctor but also a true leader.

Correcting Errors
p.38

1 The mechanic can repair **broken** cars very quickly.

2 Frankly **speaking**, I didn't do my homework.

3 **Being tired**, she just went home early.

4 **The woman sitting** on that chair looks sad.

5 The play was so **touching**, so I was **moved**.

6 The unexpected gift was **surprising**.

7 Look at that **cat sleeping** peacefully on the roof.

8 **Having drunk(en)** too much coffee in the evening, he couldn't sleep at all at night.

Chapter **4**

수동태

UNIT 07 수동태의 형태

Simple Test
p.40

1 This book <u>was</u> <u>written</u> by an unknown author.

2 This washing machine will not <u>be</u> <u>used</u> any more.

3 The final <u>is</u> <u>being</u> played now.

4 Using calculators <u>has</u> never <u>been</u> allowed in my class.

5 The bridge <u>was</u> <u>being</u> destroyed by the enemy.

Practice Test
p.41

1 The World Cup is held every four years.

2 A lot of (= Lots of) lettuce has been grown on his farm since last year.

3 Over one hundred songs were composed by the songwriter.

4 Five minutes were given to them to escape.

5 The heavy bed was being moved by four men.

6 Your new computer will be delivered by Friday.

7 Were the deer hunted by the starving lion?

8 Her letter has been kept in my drawer for ten years.

9 Thousands of dolls are made in this factory by the workers.

10 When was the key found by Luna?

Actual Test

p.42

1 Let the sheep be fed well.

2 Let it be done without any mistake.

3 Will their plan be accomplished at once?

4 May Spanish be used here?

5 This company's strollers are being made [manufactured] in China.

6 Electric cars are being sold at high prices.

7 Hope was seen in the dark.

8 The song has never been played by anybody.

9 This viola has been played by many musicians before.

10 This novel has been loved by many Koreans since last winter.

UNIT 08 여러 가지 수동태

Simple Test

p.43

1 A small bag was bought for me by him.

2 I was made happy by your smile.

3 I was not allowed to have another chance.

Practice Test

p.44

1 I was made to exercise every day by my dad.

2 That David doesn't like swimming is said by them.

3 The song was thought to be very beautiful by him.

4 A lot of money was given to his son by him.

5 It is said by them that those pearls are expensive.

6 Olivia was given a flower by Luke.

7 Good information was provided to us by them.

8 The baby was seen to crawl into the kitchen by me.

9 A tablet PC was bought for Jack by me.

10 He was heard to play the guitar by me.

Actual Test

p.45

1 He is called Red by people.

2 She was made to follow him by the teacher.

3 Tom was made to get up early in the morning by Jerry.

4 Emily was seen to walk to school by Brian.

5 The kids were seen to enter the building by Sarah.

6 It is said that Korea is a beautiful country.

7 Korea is said to be a beautiful country.

8 She was advised to come on time by John.

9 She was seen to play the piano by us.

10 Ken was made to sign the contract by Ben.

Paragraph Writing

p.47

Model Answer

Smartphones, Subways and Grandmothers

1 **It is natural that the old should be respected and taken care of.** Everyone knows that Korea is called as "the country of courteous people in the East". Therefore, it's necessary that the old are bowed to by the young.

2 These days, **smartphones are used by many people.** But this convenient device has made some problems. **Smartphones are used by many people on the subway. They are used from the beginning to the end of their trip,** so people only look at their smartphones.

3 One day, an old woman got on the subway.

No empty seats were seen, and no seats were offered, either. It was because everyone was dozing or concentrating on their smartphones.

4 **This was not because they were rude but because they never looked up as they were attracted by their smartphones.** The old woman could not expect anybody to get up because [as, since] no one noticed her.

5 This situation is wrong. **The old must be taken care of first. We should not be captured by our smartphones on the subway.** Humans are more important than a machine. Besides, they are the old and we must respect them.

Correcting Errors
p.48

1 Several people **were picked** as new staffs by the director.
2 Good restaurants should **be known** to many people.
3 The house **had** been burned out before the firefighters arrived.
4 Let them **be informed** about the meeting at once.
5 A lot of money **were donated** to the local charity.
6 He was made **to study** hard by the strict teacher.
7 **It is said** that Leo is very good at shooting with his left foot.
8 Jogging in the morning **is said to** be good for health.

Chapter **5**

접속사

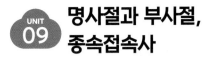

명사절과 부사절, 종속접속사
UNIT 09

Simple Test
p.50

1 My desire is that she gets to know him well.
2 He wonders whether [if] she likes him or not.
3 While his mother was cutting the rice cake, Seokbong was writing letters.
4 Why do you believe she is innocent?

Practice Test
p.51

1 I know that he is an optimist.
2 She doesn't know whether he will accept her proposal (or not).
3 He will put down the cup after he drinks the warm tea.
4 If he postpones his concert, his fans will be disappointed. (= His fans will be disappointed if he postpones his concert.)
5 Though it rained, they played soccer. (= They played soccer though it rained.)
6 After the accident occurred, the government changed the law. (= The government changed the law after the accident occurred.)
7 It is incredible that he invented this machine.
8 Who do you think will pick you up?
9 Where he stayed yesterday is not important.
10 Who found the treasure is the key point of this book.

Actual Test
p.52

1 The teacher was upset since nobody knew the answer. (= Since nobody knew the answer, the teacher was upset.)
2 As the singer's remake versions were fresh, many people liked them. (= Many people liked the singer's remake versions as they were fresh.)
3 Because his love is pure, it will not change

easily. (= His love will not change easily because it is pure.)

4 What he commands is our duty today.

5 He composed that beautiful song although he had no instruments. (= Although he had no instruments, he composed that beautiful song.)

6 That the criminal is David's younger brother is shocking. (= It is shocking that the criminal is David's younger brother.)

7 Nobody knows if they moved your cheese (or not).

8 What do you think his nickname is?

9 Unless you take these photos, I will throw them away. (= I will throw them away unless you take these photos.)

10 It is true that he eats instant noodles every day.

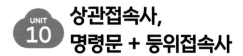

UNIT 10 상관접속사, 명령문 + 등위접속사

Simple Test
p.53

1 Weep not for me but for yourself.
2 David is good at not only English but also music.
3 Either your roommate or you have to clean the room.

Practice Test
p.54

1 Both Smith and you are my good friends.
2 Not only she but (also) I need career counseling.
3 Not you but Ken has to catch the ball.
4 Hyenas are afraid of neither lions nor leopards.
5 Both the employer and the employees are responsible for the strike.
6 My uncle is not only a poet but (also) a painter.
7 Listen carefully, and you will get the point.
8 If you listen carefully, you will get the

point. (= You will get the point if you listen carefully.)

9 Make sure to check if you have the camera, or you will not (= won't) take (any) pictures.

10 Unless you make sure to check if you have the camera, you will not (= won't) take (any) pictures.

Actual Test
p.55

1 Amelia keeps not only her own dog but (also) abandoned dogs.
2 Amelia keeps abandoned dogs as well as her own dog.
3 He was not an enemy but one of our soldiers.
4 Both faith and love are very important in our lives.
5 Either you or he has to tell her the truth.
6 Neither Minho nor Minsu has lived in England.
7 This food is neither delicious nor cheap.
8 Not only his right-footed shots but (also) the left-footed ones [shots] were accurate.
9 Read a lot of books, and your mind will be fertile.
10 Love one another, or you will quarrel.

Paragraph Writing
p.57

Model Answer

My Friend with the Nickname "Library"

1 **It is obvious that** everyone wants to have a good nickname. Here is a story of my friend Seongmin. He earned the nickname "Library" **because** he loved reading **when** he was young. He preferred reading books to playing games. We called him "Library" **because** we could always find him there.

2 He has now become a writer who has written a lot of books. He **not only** reads the books **but also** buys them. There are so many books in his house. **After** he finishes reading one book, he starts writing

a new book. He seems to know everything. He recommends trying different types of books and authors to make reading more interesting.

3 Seongmin leads a reading club called EWB (Enjoy with Books). Many people read various books, share their opinions, and even create new stories. **Although** he is busy, he has never missed a reading club meeting.

4 My friend Seongmin has become a famous writer **not only** in Korea **but also** in many other countries. Through reading various books and building relationships with people, he gains new energy and continuously develops himself. I am proud to have such a friend.

Correcting Errors   p.58

1 **That** he is very kind to all the people is well known.

2 Nobody knows **if [whether]** he comes today or not.

3 **What** do you think the most expensive car in the world is?

4 **Though [Although, Even though]** the weather was terrible, they could finish the wedding ceremony outside.

5 Both his mom and he **were** satisfied with their friendly service.

6 Not the color but the price **was** suitable for him.

7 You as well as she **are** a good student for the teacher.

8 Practice hard every day, **and** you will be a good singer.

Chapter 6

관계사

UNIT
11 관계부사

Simple Test   p.60

1 This is the <u>reason</u> <u>why</u> I like Terry.
2 Tell me the <u>time</u> <u>when</u> he will come.
3 This is the <u>place</u> <u>where</u> the band performed.
4 He showed her <u>the</u> <u>way</u> he fixed the machine.

Practice Test   p.61

1 This is the town where he painted the famous painting.
2 Do you know the reason (why) he ran away?
3 The mother bird taught the baby birds how they could fly.
4 I know the year when he debuted.
5 Memorial Day is a day when almost every shop closes.
6 The reason (why) she is angry is not clear.
7 Who can forget the day when thirty-three independence fighters fought against Japan?
8 This is the building where my father works.
9 This is the neighborhood where he got lost last week.
10 She knows well the way siblings treat each other [one another].

Actual Test   p.62

1 We went to the museum, where we saw Walter.

2 She told me a secret last Saturday, when we were watching a movie.

3 I went to the amusement park, where I met Rachel.

4 Tomorrow is Sunday, when he will (= is going to) go to the museum.

5 Late at night is the best time when she can read books.

6 Let me know how you memorize words so well.

7 This is the place where many (= a lot of = lots of) soldiers sacrificed themselves in the war.

8 Last week when she had an audition was fantastic.

9 The boss didn't tell me the reason (why) he fired me.

10 I went to the hospital, where the nurse gave me a shot.

UNIT 12 복합관계대명사, 복합관계부사

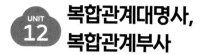

Simple Test
p.63

1 <u>Whatever</u> you do, I trust you.

2 <u>Whenever</u> I miss you, I close my eyes.

3 <u>Whoever</u> comes here will be welcomed.

4 You may choose <u>whichever</u> you want.

Practice Test
p.64

1 There is no place like home however humble it is. (= However humble it is, there is no place like home. = There is no place like home no matter how humble it is. = No matter how humble it is, there is no place like home.)

2 Please call me whenever you need my help. (= Whenever you need my help, please call me.)

3 Andy will be able to succeed wherever he goes. (= Wherever he goes, Andy will be able to succeed.)

4 Don't give up however hard this problem is. (= However hard this problem is, don't give up. = Don't give up no matter how hard this problem is. = No matter how hard this problem is, don't give up.)

5 I will give this present to whoever wants it. (= I will give this present to anyone who wants it.)

6 We will defeat the enemy soldiers wherever they appear. (= Wherever the enemy soldiers appear, we will defeat them. = We will defeat the enemy soldiers no matter where they appear. = No matter where they appear, we will defeat them.)

7 Whoever believes me will win the game. (= Anyone who believes me will win the game.)

8 Whoever breaks the rules will be kicked out. (= Anyone who breaks the rules will be kicked out.)

9 We can climb the castle however high it is. (= However high the castle is, we can climb it. = We can climb the castle no matter how high it is. = No matter how high the castle is, we can climb it.)

10 We need whoever can drive a car. (= We need anyone who can drive a car.)

Actual Test
p.65

1 Whoever hears the news will be shocked.

2 Whatever you eat will be delicious.

3 Whoever answers this question may go home.

4 However little he has, he is willing to share it. (= He is willing to share it however little he has. = No matter how little he has, he is willing to share it.)

5 He sent me on an errand whenever I visited him. (= Whenever I visited him, he sent me on an errand.)

6 Whatever my mom cooks is delicious.

7 We deliver whatever you order.

8 The cafeteria served Jajangmyeon for lunch whenever she wore a white shirt.

(= Whenever she wore a white shirt, the cafeteria served Jajangmyeon for lunch.)

9 Whoever envies others is a failure.

10 You have to finish this report by tomorrow however tired you may be. (= However tired you may be, you have to finish this report by tomorrow. = You have to finish this report no matter how tired you may be. = No matter how tired you may be, you have to finish this report.)

Paragraph Writing
p.67

Model Answer
Same Word, Different Meaning

1 There are a lot of English words which have various meanings. A few words even seem to have two meanings that are the opposite of each other.

2 Whenever we look in the dictionary, we don't know which meaning to choose. (= We don't know which meaning to choose whenever we look in the dictionary.) There are many words that have ten or more meanings. **This is the reason why I sometimes get confused for a minute.**

3 For example, the words such as "make, take, to, and for" have many meanings. And the word "leave" has two meanings that seem to be the opposite of each other. "Leave" can mean "to depart", and it can also mean "to remain".

4 "Did he leave Seoul?" means "Did he depart from Seoul?" and "Did he leave something?" means "Did he put something down which is still there now?" **Whichever the meaning is, most of the time people don't get too confused.** (= Most of the time people don't get too confused whichever the meaning is.) **However hard it is, we usually figure it out.** (= We usually figure it out however hard it is.)

5 For example, we will know whether "Fine for parking" means "A good place to park"

or "A penalty for parking in this place" after we get a parking ticket.

Correcting Errors
p.68

1 I can't forget the place **where [at which]** I had the first interview.

2 Let me know **the way** I get to the station by car. (= Let me know **how** I get to the station by car.)

3 Do you remember the day **when [on which]** we played soccer in the heavy rain?

4 We went to a big zoo, **where** we saw many special animals.

5 Can you tell me the reason **why** you were absent for school yesterday?

6 **However tired you are**, you had better take a shower.

7 Whatever the inventor makes **is** creative all the time.

8 No **matter** where you stay, it can be your shelter.

Chapter 7

가정법

UNIT 13
가정법 과거,
가정법 과거완료

Simple Test
p.70

1 If I <u>were</u> you, I <u>would</u> tell her.
2 If I <u>had</u> enough time, I <u>could</u> go there.
3 If I <u>had</u> <u>had</u> a camera, I <u>would</u> <u>have</u> taken many pictures.
4 If they <u>had</u> won the game, they <u>wouldn't</u> <u>have</u> been disappointed.

Practice Test
p.71

1 If I were Superman, I would fly there right now. (= I would fly there right now if I were Superman.)

2 If you talked to her more kindly, she would have more confidence. (= She would have more confidence if you talked to her more kindly.)

3 If Richard had won the contest, he would have been happy. (= He would have been happy if Richard had won the contest.)

4 If Paul had played the guitar well, Julie would have fallen in love with him. (= Julie would have fallen in love with him if Paul had played the guitar well.)

5 If I had a dictionary, I would look up the words. (= I would look up the words if I had a dictionary.)

6 If we had taken the subway, we wouldn't have been late. (= We wouldn't have been late if we had taken the subway.)

7 If the soccer player were here, he could show us his fantastic free kicks. (= The soccer player could show us his fantastic free kicks if he were here.)

8 If the singer were alive, we could listen to more of his beautiful songs. (= We could listen to more of his beautiful songs if the singer were alive.)

9 If this house were mine, I would paint this dark wall a bright color. (= I would paint this dark wall a bright color if this house were mine.)

10 If she had sung better songs, she would have been a more popular singer. (= She would have been a more popular singer if she had sung better songs.)

Actual Test
p.72

1 If she had read many books, she could have learned more words. (= She could have learned more words if she had read many books.)

2 If the boy hadn't thrown the ball, the window wouldn't have broken. (= The window wouldn't have broken if the boy hadn't thrown the ball.)

3 If I were invisible, I could go anywhere. (= I could go anywhere if I were invisible.)

4 If I were tall, I could dunk the ball in front of her. (= I could dunk the ball in front of her if I were tall.)

5 If my older sister were my math teacher, I would ask her difficult questions. (= I would ask her difficult questions if my older sister were my math teacher.)

6 If I were a good chef, I would cook her a delicious dinner. (= I would cook a delicious dinner for her if I were a good chef.)

7 If his name had been on the list, we would have been happy. (= We would have been happy if his name had been on the list.)

8 If it snowed now, I would make a snowman and call it Olaf. (= I would make a snowman and call it Olaf if it snowed now.)

9 If I were a butterfly, I would have beautiful wings. (= I would have beautiful wings if I were a butterfly.)

10 If there were twenty-five hours in a day, I could sleep an hour longer. (= I could sleep an hour longer if there were twenty-five hours in a day.)

UNIT 14 여러 가지 가정법

Simple Test
p.73

1 I wish I were the CEO of the entertainment company.

2 Tony talks as if he liked me.

Practice Test
p.74

1 I wish (that) he had had a good time with his family.

2 I wish (that) I were as tall as you.

3 I wish (that) you had had a hamburger in Switzerland.

4 He talked as if he had seen [watched] the movie several times.

5 She stopped walking as if she had heard some strange sounds.

6 I wish (that) I could look after those poor children.

7 She looks as if she had not eaten anything for a few days.

8 I wish (that) you had brought your younger brother.

9 He talks as if he could speak five languages.

10 He acted as if he had not been the captain of the team.

Actual Test
p.75

1 If it were not for the mist, I could drive faster. (= I could drive faster if it were not for the mist.)

2 Without electricity, we would be very uncomfortable.

3 If it had not been for kimchi, we couldn't have eaten [had] dinner. (= We couldn't have eaten [had] dinner if it had not been for kimchi.)

4 But for his giving her a ride, she would have been late for school.

5 Without email, we couldn't have conducted the survey.

6 He spoke as if it had been a secret.

7 She acts as though she were a millionaire.

8 He pretended as if he had studied music in college.

9 I wish (that) I were dreaming at this moment.

10 If it were not for the laws, people would act as they like. (= People would act as they like if it were not for the laws.)

Paragraph Writing
p.77

Model Answer

If I were...

1 If I were the wind, in the summer I would blow cool air for you.
Like a refreshing breeze on a hot day, I would blow cool air for you.

2 If I were a cloud, I would rain moistly for you.
Like a welcome rain on a dry land, I would rain for you.

3 If I were a big tree, I would make some shade for you.
To rest your tired body and heart, I would make some shade for you.

4 If I were a big rock, I would be a bench for you.
To let you sit comfortably after a hard day, I would be a bench for you.

5 I talk as if I were nature. I talk as if I were free.

Correcting Errors
p.78

1 If I **were** you, I would give her a special present.

2 I wish I **could** donate a lot of money to the poor.

3 If it **were** not for the air, nobody could breathe every day.

4 She talks as if she **had known** everything about science.

5 If I had been rich at that time, I **could have helped** them.

6 They always speak **as though [if]** they were experts.

7 **But for** their support, I **wouldn't have overcome** the challenges.

8 If you had concentrated on the project, you **could have finished** it quickly.

Chapter 8

일치와 화법

UNIT 15 수의 일치, 시제 일치의 예외

Simple Test   p.80

1 Every student is present.
2 Three years is not too long a time to wait for him.
3 Logics is hard to understand.

Practice Test   p.81

1 Everyone needs water.
2 *Romeo and Juliet* is this week's best-seller at this bookstore.
3 Mathematics is a very difficult subject for me.
4 A number of scientists were invited to the White House.
5 Half of the building is hers.
6 Half of the buildings are very beautiful.
7 My father told me that time is gold.
8 She will tell her daughter that Mozart composed many good songs.
9 Bread and jam is very good for breakfast.
10 Most of this money is Billy's.

Actual Test   p.82

1 Every person wants to live happily.
2 Two hundred dollars is a high price for this bicycle [bike].
3 The United States consists of fifty states.
4 Two kilometers is a very short distance to go by car.
5 The young have to work hard for their future.

6 Linguistics has several branches.
7 The child learned yesterday that the sun rises in the east.
8 I know that the Korean War broke out in 1950.
9 She said that she goes to bed at 10 every night.
10 Every housewife in this town shops at the local farmers' market.

UNIT 16 화법

Practice Test   p.84

1 ① She said to me, "You look tired today."
  ② She told me that I looked tired that day.
2 ① Ryan said to her, "I was late for school yesterday."
  ② Ryan told her that he had been late for school the previous day.
3 ① He asked me, "Are you hungry?"
  ② He asked me if [whether] I was hungry.
4 ① I asked him, "How did you know that?"
  ② I asked him how he had known that.
5 ① She told him, "Don't park (your car) here."
  ② She ordered him not to park (his car) there.

Actual Test   p.85

1 Jane asked him where he was from.
2 Sally told him that she liked classical music.
3 Mom asked me where I had been the previous day.
4 She asked me what I would eat the next day.
5 David advised her not to give up.
6 The police officer suggested to them that they should follow the truck.
7 The teacher advised me not to get angry so easily.
8 He proposed our going to the sea then.
9 She told me that she had lost her purse the previous day.
10 He asked me if I had been tired then.

Paragraph Writing

p.87

Model Answer

Looking Back Today...

1 Today, I ended my relationship with Cindy, one of my close friends. It is hard to end a relationship with close friends, but this morning I was shocked.

2 **Becky told me (that) Cindy liked my boyfriend Steve.** I couldn't believe it. Then I saw Steve and Cindy smiling and talking with each other. I was so angry that **I suggested to Cindy that we should end our relationship.**

3 **I told her (that) I never wanted to talk to her again.** I came home after school, and I was confused, **so I told my older sister Jane what had happened.**

4 As soon as Jane heard my story, **she smiled and told me (that) Cindy and Steve went to the same church and that they were doing a play together. She said (that) she had seen them practicing together. She said (that) they had been practicing for that play. Steve told me (that) he was in a church play,** but I didn't know Cindy did the same play.

5 I will apologize to her tomorrow. I can't wait for tomorrow morning.

Correcting Errors

p.88

1 Every **person has** their own unique talents.

2 Each **case needs** more witnesses to the accident.

3 The number of the participants **was** only five.

4 She asked me **what my email address is.**

5 The teacher ordered me **not to forget** my homework again.

6 He asked me **if [whether]** I was hungry or not.

7 John proposed **my joining** the team today.

8 A number of **students** gathered in the library

to study for their exams.

Chapter 9

특수 구문

UNIT 17 강조, 부분 부정

Simple Test

p.90

1 He <u>did</u> finish the work within three hours.

2 This is <u>the</u> <u>very</u> history book that I was looking for.

3 It was at <u>Lisa's</u> <u>house</u> that they had a party.

4 I <u>should</u> <u>have</u> said goodbye to my grandmother.

Practice Test

p.91

1 I do want to be the MVP in this competition.

2 Her choice is not always a good choice.

3 It was Susan that bought coffee at the store yesterday.

4 It was coffee that Susan bought at the store yesterday.

5 It was at the store that Susan bought coffee yesterday.

6 It was yesterday that Susan bought coffee at the store.

7 You should have followed his directions here.

8 He must have sent many people invitations. (= He must have sent invitations to many people.)

9 He did score the winning goal in the final of the Champions League.

10 Who in the world stole your shoes?

Actual Test

p.92

1 It was the museum that we went to last week.
2 It was last week that we went to the museum.
3 It was us that went to the museum last week.
4 Jessica did write a letter to Bill Gates. (= Jessica did write Bill Gates a letter.)
5 How on earth did you open the door without your keys?
6 This is the very moment that I was hoping for.
7 Children's opinions are not (= aren't) always wrong.
8 They should have abandoned the work earlier.
9 They must have done nothing yesterday.
10 All soldiers are not brave.

UNIT 18 도치

Simple Test

p.93

1 Under the tree was Jackson reading a book.
2 Here comes Sally.
3 Were I rich, I would help many poor people.
4 Not a single word did she say after hearing the news.

Practice Test

p.94

1 Little did I expect her to visit my office.
2 Not only is she smart, but (she is) also beautiful.
3 May they return home safe!
4 Here comes the bus that we have to take.
5 Had I been there, I could have helped you.
6 Not a single cup of Coke did he drink.
7 Hardly ever can we see they play a live concert.
8 On the hill stood a white house.
9 Not until she came could we start the meeting.
10 Never have I seen such a tall man.

Actual Test

p.95

1 Hardly ever does she lose her temper.
2 Were I you, I would tell her the truth.
3 Never have I been to England.
4 Not until midnight did the store close.
5 Hardly were they able to recognize the danger ahead of them.
6 Not until he came to Korea did he learn Korean.
7 Never have I seen such a severe storm.
8 Not until this morning did it stop raining.
9 May God bless you!
10 Seldom is Daniel late for school.

Paragraph Writing

p.97

Model Answer

I Should Have Studied Harder!

1 The final exam was today. But I did terrible. One month before the exam, I started my preparations for the exam. But I didn't prepare enough. **I shouldn't have played computer games.** I spent more time playing games rather than studying.
2 Whenever I play games, I can concentrate well. (= I can concentrate well whenever I play games.) But when I study, I can't. **It was because of a lack of a sense of purpose that I couldn't concentrate on studying.**
3 When I play a computer game, my purpose is to break my record score. (= My purpose is to break my record score when I play a computer game.) But when I study, I don't have a purpose. (= I don't have a purpose when I study.) **I should have studied harder. Not until the end of the exam did**

I realize the importance of having a clear purpose. What on earth was I thinking?

4 For the next exam, I will have a purpose. Now I know how to succeed, I am sure I will do well on the next test.

Correcting Errors
p.98

1 He **did love** Stella with all his heart.
2 It was at the park **that [where]** I first rode a bicycle.
3 I lost my wallet. I **should have been** careful.
4 Hardly **did he do** his homework. The homeroom teacher would call his mom.
5 Here **comes the bus** to the bus stop.
6 He didn't prepare the presentation. He **must have been** busy.
7 This is **the** very place where I really wanted to come.
8 **Were I** a famous movie star, I could take part in the Movie Awards.

Final Test 1
p.100

1 Whatever he says, I can't trust him.
2 Not until the summer did he lose weight.
3 Not knowing the news, she was very confused.
4 Not only you but she is their relative.
5 Frankly [Honestly] speaking, this food is not delicious.
6 Not having seen her before, he was nervous.
7 The building is being completed by this company.
8 This is the town where my grandfather was born.
9 Tell me the way you made this.
10 She must not have known the fact.
11 He should have thrown the ball far away.
12 Not having enough time to do it well, he finished it quickly.
13 Not she but you are his older sister.
14 Let it be stayed there.

15 I wish she were my friend.
16 He looked as if he had been very tired.
17 If I were a child, I could have many toys.
18 Whatever you say, I will do it.
19 No matter what you do, do your best.
20 Whoever marries him will be happy.

Final Test 2
p.102

1 If I were a butterfly, I would land on flowers. (= I would land on flowers if I were a butterfly.)
2 If it had been money, I would have picked it up. (= I would have picked it up if it had been money.)
3 I wish (that) I could speak English like a native speaker.
4 He talks as if he were a baby.
5 Physics is my favorite subject.
6 He explained (that) the Earth revolves around the Sun.
7 She asked me what my hobby was.
8 The broken dish was Mom's favorite one.
9 Listening to music, he washed [did] the dishes. (– He washed [did] the dishes, listening to music.)
10 Strictly speaking, she didn't do her homework by herself.
11 Neither you nor she needs his help.
12 Her wish is that every child in the world eats well.
13 Was the novel read by you?
14 A huge pizza is being made by the cook.
15 He has been writing the book for three months.
16 Tell me the time when I depart from here.
17 Not until lunchtime could she sit down.
18 What on earth did they do in the office?
19 Every person wants to be loved.
20 If it were not for money, Daniel couldn't buy anything. (= Daniel couldn't buy anything if it were not for money.)

MEMO